Silas

Marmee

One-Minute Devotions® for Boys

Text copyright © 2010 by Jayce O'Neal
All rights reserved.

Developed in co-operation with Educational Publishing Concepts.

© 2011 Christian Art Gifts Inc., IL, USA
        Christian Art Publishers, RSA

First Faux Leather edition 2016

Editor: Linda Taylor

Cover designed by Christian Art Publishers

Images used under license from Shutterstock.com

Scripture quotations marked NIV are taken from the *Holy Bible*,
New International Version® NIV®. Copyright © 1973, 1978, 1984
by International Bible Society. Used by permission of Zondervan
Publishing House. All rights reserved.

Scripture quotations marked NLT are taken from the *Holy Bible*,
New Living Translation, second edition. Copyright © 1996, 2004
by Tyndale House Publishers, Carol Stream, Illinois 60188.
All rights reserved.

Printed in China

ISBN 978-1-4321-1723-8

© All rights reserved. No part of this book may be reproduced in any
form without permission in writing from the publisher, except in the
case of brief quotations embodied in critical articles or reviews.

21 22 23 24 25 26 27 28 29 30 – 15 14 13 12 11 10 9 8 7 6

Printed in Shenzhen, China
DEC 2021
Print Run: PUR402145

one-minute DEVOTIONS for Boys

Jayce O'Neal

CHRISTIAN ART PUBLISHERS

JANUARY

WHAT SMART PEOPLE DO (WISDOM FROM PROVERBS)

HOW TO GET SMART

The fear of the LORD is the beginning
of knowledge, but fools despise wisdom
and discipline. (Proverbs 1:7, NIV)

Sometimes people do not really understand what this verse means. Smart people fear God. However, this is not the kind of fear you have for a mean person. God is not mean. This kind of fear means that you have a strong respect and love for God. The more you respect and love him, the more you want to do what he wants you to do.

God's ways are always better than your own. He says that when you do respect his ways, you are starting to be smarter than you were when you only did what you wanted.

People who aren't smart don't like wisdom; they only want to do things their own way. So be smarter than other people by respecting God.

Dear God, please help me to be wise and respect you as I should. Amen.

DISCIPLINE = LOVE

*My son, do not despise the LORD's discipline
and do not resent his rebuke, because the LORD
disciplines those he loves. (Proverbs 3:11-12, NIV)*

If you stole some money from your mom's purse,
your parents might ground you for a month. Your
parents would discipline you because they love
you and want you to become a good person who
loves God. They punish you so you will not do
things that will get you into even worse trouble
later on.

If you steal something when you are an adult
you could go to jail, so it is better to learn that
lesson now instead of later. God's discipline is
like that. Because he loves you, he wants you to
live life the right way. Sometimes you might not
always want to do the right thing, but God knows
that a little pain now for doing something wrong
is better than a lot of pain later.

Lord, thank you for loving me so much that you discipline me for my own good. Amen.

TELLING THE TRUTH

Don't pick a fight without reason, when no one has done you harm. (Proverbs 3:30, NLT)

When Jesus was arrested, some of the Pharisees paid men to tell lies about Jesus. They had to pay people to lie because they could not find anyone who could say anything bad about Jesus without making it up. Jesus was a perfect man, so there were no real bad things to say about him.

Can you imagine if you were in Jesus' shoes and people were lying, saying you did bad things when you didn't? It would not be fun. That is why God does not want you tell lies about other people. God doesn't like lying, but especially when it gets someone who is innocent into trouble.

God, help me to watch the things I say about other people. Amen.

MAKING MOM SMILE

A wise child brings joy to a father; a foolish child brings grief to a mother. (Proverbs 10:1, NLT)

You remember the story of Jesus' crucifixion? He hung on a cross with two thieves crucified on either side of him. One of the thieves believed that Jesus was the Messiah, but the other one didn't. The thief who did believe got to go to heaven, but the other guy didn't. It must have been tough for the thief who denied Jesus, but what about his parents? That man had a mom and dad too, but he made a bunch of bad decisions and probably made his mom cry.

When you listen to God's wisdom, you make your parents proud; if you ignore them, it doesn't just hurt you, but it also hurts everyone who loves you. Don't be like that thief on the cross who didn't trust in Jesus. Live more like Jesus. He made his mom Mary proud.

Jesus, help me to be a joy to my parents by being wise. Amen.

WISE WORKER

A wise youth harvests in the summer,
but one who sleeps during harvest is
a disgrace. (Proverbs 10:5, NLT)

To play soccer, you have to work hard. If one player worked really hard and did everything the coach asked him to and another player was lazy, then you would expect the coach to play the hard-working player, right? Since players reflect the coach, then the coach would want a hard worker. This is true with God, too. He wants his children to work hard because they are reflections of him.

Those who work hard will be ready when the big game comes. Those who are lazy won't get very far. God wants you to be a hard worker because you reflect him. He wants you to be prepared when the time is right.

God, please give me the strength to work hard no matter what. Amen.

MOTOR MOUTHS

The wise in heart accept commands, but a chattering fool comes to ruin. (Proverbs 10:8, NIV)

When people get caught doing something they shouldn't, they generally do one of two things. They might admit what they have done wrong and learn from what their parents, teachers, or pastors have to say, or they might ramble off a million excuses to try to justify the wrong things they did.

A smart kid admits his mistake, learns from it, and moves on. The next time he is tempted to do the same thing, he can avoid it by listening to the wise words of adults. If he is a motor mouth and tries to excuse his wrong deeds, then he will likely make the same mistakes over and over again. God does not reward a chattering fool. Instead, God rewards those with open hearts who are willing to learn from their mistakes.

God, please help me to listen to people who are smarter than me, even when I think I know everything. Amen.

TIGHT-LIPPED

*Too much talk leads to sin. Be sensible and
keep your mouth shut. (Proverbs 10:19, NLT)*

Talking isn't a bad thing, but talking too much
can lead to bad things. When you are at school
and your friends are talking about other people, it
can be easy to say something bad about someone
because you want to feel part of the group or get
a laugh. God warns you to be very careful in what
you say because your words can be very powerful.
If you have ever been yelled at or been called a
mean name, then you know how painful words
can be.

When you speak, remember the wise saying,
"If you can't say something nice, don't say anything at all." One of the greatest signs of godly
wisdom is knowing when to talk and when not
to talk.

God, help me to know when to talk and when to be
quiet. Amen.

TROUBLEMAKERS

A fool finds pleasure in evil conduct,
but a man of understanding delights
in wisdom. (Proverbs 10:23, NIV)

Some people just like to cause trouble. Lucifer was the most beautiful angel of all before he fell from heaven and became the devil, Satan. Now, he looks for other troublemakers to cause as many problems as possible. If you love God, then you want to stay away from the devil and his friends. To do this, you must decide not to surround yourself with friends who like trouble. If your friends are always coming up with plans to cause problems, then you need to choose new friends.

If you stay around troublemakers too long, then you often start to think like they do. The devil took a third of the angels with him to wage a war against God. Don't let troublemakers influence you. To be God's friend means to choose your other friends wisely.

Jesus, help me to choose my friends carefully. Amen.

BADGE OF HONOR

Avoiding a fight is a mark of honor; only fools insist on quarreling. (Proverbs 20:3, NLT)

Some kids at school might try to convince you that to be cool you have to fight, but God's definition of cool is much different than what the kids at school think. God doesn't see people who like to fight as cool, but rather as fools.

If someone tries to get you to fight and argue, ignore him. Avoiding fights is not wimpy, but rather the opposite. It takes more strength to avoid fighting than it does to get into a fist fight. Remember that avoiding conflict is a badge of honor in God's eyes, no matter what other kids might think or say.

Jesus, please guide my actions so that I avoid quarrels. Help me to be uplifting to others. Amen.

PLAYING FAIR

The LORD detests the use of dishonest scales, but he delights in accurate weights. (Proverbs 11:1, NLT)

Winning a game is fun. When you work hard to do something well, it is exciting when God rewards your effort. But if you win by cheating, then not only is it *not* fun, but God will not reward you. God is a God of justice. He delights in what's right, but if you cheat, then you are doing something that God hates.

You probably desire to please God, so do your best to always play by the rules and be fair to those you play against. If you play team soccer or even a game of frisbee or tag in your neighborhood, be sure to play fairly with everyone.

Lord, help me to be fair and honest in all that I do. Amen.

BE HONEST

Honesty guides good people; dishonesty destroys treacherous people. (Proverbs 11:3, NLT)

When Judas betrayed Jesus, he felt guilty for it afterward. He did not know where to turn. He went to the Pharisees who had paid him to betray Jesus, but they rejected him. Judas's story ends tragically. Because of his shame, he never went to Jesus for help; instead, he went away and killed himself.

Those who live to do wrong always end up lost at some point. Dishonesty clouds people's eyes so they don't know where to go. Ultimately, just as the Bible says, it destroys them. However, if you have godly honesty, the Holy Spirit will guide you.

Judas could have turned to Jesus and made everything right by asking forgiveness, but he didn't. Do your best to live with honesty, but if you mess up, turn to Jesus as soon as possible.

Dear Father, please give me direction and help me not to get lost. Amen.

WISE ADVICE

Without wise leadership, a nation falls; there is safety in having many advisers. (Proverbs 11:14, NLT)

All people need to have good friends who tell them like it is. David was king of Israel, but he did not always make good decisions. He desired another man's wife and was even responsible for the death of her husband. Nathan the prophet confronted David. Even though Nathan told David he had done wrong, David listened to his wise counsel. As a result, David repented to God for all of his mistakes.

If Nathan had been afraid to speak up or if David had ignored him, then David's mistakes would have been even bigger. Just because someone doesn't agree with you does not mean he is wrong. Sometimes you need people who disagree with you – especially to point out if you are making mistakes. Like David, be willing to listen to other people's wise advice.

God, I pray that you will surround me with wise people who can give me good advice. Amen.

CLOSER THAN A BROTHER

Many will say they are loyal friends, but who can find one who is truly reliable? (Proverbs 20:6, NLT)

The Bible says that Jesus will stick closer than a brother, so you can always count on him no matter what you go through in life. This is important because, in life, people may disappoint you from time to time. Parents, friends, and teachers all make mistakes. Sometimes those you think are your friends let you down by lying about you, not defending you when they should, or leaving you to hang out with other friends.

No matter how people disappoint you, you should always aim to do what is right. Your actions are between you and God, and not everyone else. Even when others hurt or ignore you, it is your job to do what is right. Remember that you can always count on Jesus.

Father, thank you for always being there for me. In tough times, please remind me of your presence. Amen.

LASTING TREASURE

Whoever trusts in his riches will fall,
but the righteous will thrive like a
green leaf. (Proverbs 11:28, NIV)

When you watch TV, you often see celebrities putting their trust in the money they have made and the power of influence that their fame has given them. However, all that stuff can easily fade away at any given moment. Those famous people can't take those riches with them when they die.

If your life is not in line with God's word, everything – including money – is meaningless. This is why God wants you to be righteous. To be righteous is to do what is right through your actions and in your heart. When you trust in God's promises, he will bless you and help you to grow, just like Proverbs says!

Jesus, help me to trust in you and your ways and not in money. Amen.

FAMILY FUN

*He who brings trouble on his family will in-
herit only wind, and the fool will be servant
to the wise. (Proverbs 11:29, NIV)*

One of God's greatest gifts is family. Families
help you up when you're down and cheer you
on when you succeed. There are all sorts of families. Some have two parents, others adopt special
needs kids, and some are not even legally related
but are closely-knit friends who lean on each
other.

No family is perfect. Those you love will make
mistakes from time to time. You may not always
get along, but do your best to bring peace in your
family. This might mean letting your brother or
sister sit in the front seat when you really want
to or sharing a certain toy even when it's difficult. Fools argue and, like Proverbs says, end up
serving those who are smart enough to avoid
causing trouble at home.

God, please help me not to cause trouble at home. I
want to bring peace to my family. Amen.

STREET YELLER

*Better to be a nobody and yet have a servant
than pretend to be somebody and have
no food. (Proverbs 12:9, NIV)*

Once there was a man who stood in the streets and yelled about how wonderful and successful he was. He did this every day for hours and hours, but when he left the street he had nowhere to go. Why? Because despite all his yelling about his success, he had no home and no food. He was unwilling to work because of how wonderful he thought he was.

God says in Proverbs that a man who is not famous but works hard is better than a man who promotes himself but cannot support himself. Words are cheap. Your hard work speaks louder of your success than just yelling about how awesome you think you are.

God, please help me not to praise myself, but to work hard and be humble in all I do. Amen.

CARE FOR YOUR PETS

The godly care for their animals, but the wicked are always cruel. (Proverbs 12:10, NLT)

When Adam was created, one of his main jobs was naming all of the animals. God entrusted this job to him, so Adam likely spent a lot of time with the animals. If you have pets, God has entrusted them to you, so you need to take good care of them. God loves you, but the Bible says God cares for his other creations, too.

Take care of the animals God has entrusted to your care. It was one of the first jobs God gave to humans, so it is important work. Feed them, love them, and do not abuse them.

Jesus, please show me how to treat my animals well. Amen.

LYING LIPS

The LORD detests lying lips, but he delights in men who are truthful. (Proverbs 12:22, NIV)

Ananias and his wife Sapphira gave money to the church, but they lied about how much they gave. Acts 5 tells the story about how this man and his wife died instantly because they lied about their giving. In God's eyes, there are no "little lies" or "white lies." God loves the truth and detests lying lips. "Detests" is a strong word for dislikes. You don't want God to detest your lips.

Do not fudge the truth even a little bit. God knows the whole truth, no matter what. God enjoys it when you are truthful. So always tell the truth, even when it is not easy to do so.

God, I want to tell the truth, so please help me to be truthful even when it's hard. Amen.

FOOLS RUSH IN

Stay away from fools, for you won't find knowledge on their lips. (Proverbs 14:7, NLT)

You will likely meet lots of people in your life. You will meet people at school, at church, at the local park, or at a basketball game. You may not know much about a person at first, but if you discover that he or she is not a good person to hang out with, then you should leave right away.

For example, if you meet Jacob at lunch and he starts planning how to skip school or says bad things about other people, then don't wait around ... just leave. The longer you are with such a person the greater the chance that the person's foolishness will rub off on you. If you get dragged into someone else's foolishness, you'll be in trouble, even if you never wanted to do anything wrong.

Jesus, please place me with good friends. If someone is not good for me, please help me to walk away when I should. Amen.

WATCH YOUR TEMPER

Short-tempered people do foolish things, and schemers are hated. (Proverbs 14:17, NLT)

Several times in the Bible, we read that Peter had a bit of a temper and sometimes acted foolishly. When Jesus was being arrested, Peter reacted quickly by taking a swipe at a guard's ear with a sword. Peter should have known that brute force and knee-jerk reactions were not what Jesus wanted. So even though he was being arrested, Jesus healed the guard's ear.

A short-tempered person acts quickly and does not give enough time to think about how to handle the situation wisely. When you get angry, do not react right away. Most likely, you will feel bad about it later and wish you had kept your mouth shut. Instead, when you get angry, ask God to give you patience.

Lord, when I feel angry, please give me patience. Help me to be careful about what I say and what I do. Amen.

HELPING THE POOR

He who oppresses the poor shows contempt for their Maker, but whoever is kind to the needy honors God. (Proverbs 14:31, NIV)

Jesus could have hung out with just about any-one he wanted to, but he didn't hang out with the wealthy and powerful people like the Pharisees and the Romans. Jesus spent most of his time with the poor. Jesus gave most of his attention to the sick and unpopular people because he had a special place in his heart for people who knew they needed help.

The homeless and sick are just like you – they are simply people who need love and friendship, but they also need other things, like food and shelter. God does not like it when people make fun of or ignore the poor; instead, he encourages his followers to be kind and to give to those in need.

Lord, I want to be nice to the poor, so please help me to be kind to them. Amen.

AN EXAMPLE SETTER

Godliness makes a nation great, but sin is a disgrace to any people. (Proverbs 14:34, NLT)

In the Old Testament, the Bible tells of times when Israel followed God's will and loved God, but then there were times when the nation ignored God and chose to sin. When the people obeyed God, they prospered, but when they ignored God, they suffered a lot of tough times. The same is true today. When a country obeys God's laws, he blesses that country.

You can't change everyone, but you can set an example to others by not sinning and by living God's way. Change your country one person at a time by being a good example of a kid who loves God and listens to his word.

God, help my country to stay away from doing wrong because I want us to do what is right. Show me how I can be an example of one person doing right. Amen.

HARSH WORDS

A gentle answer turns away wrath, but a harsh word stirs up anger. (Proverbs 15:1, NIV)

If your friend Josh came up to you and started yelling at you about all the things you do wrong, how would you feel? Most people would either yell back or get scared and say nothing. However, if Josh came to you gently saying he was worried about something you were doing, you probably would listen to him if you could tell that he was talking to you out of love.

When someone yells and screams mean words at you, you're not going to be interested in listening. When someone talks to you because he is concerned for you, however, it is easier to listen to what he has to say. When you speak to others, honor God by speaking gently and using words that don't stir up anger.

Father, please give me soft words and help me to speak gently even to those who are not always nice themselves. Amen.

GOOD INTENTIONS

The LORD's light penetrates the human spirit, exposing every hidden motive. (Proverbs 20:27, NLT)

Juan and Todd plan to go on a missions trip to help kids in Asia. Both seem to want to please God, but Juan wants to go because he hopes to impress a girl at church. Going on a missions trip may impress the girl, but it will not impress God. He does not just see *what* you do but also *why* you do those things.

Good deeds might look good, but if you do them for wrong reasons, you can't hide your motives from God. As Proverbs says, God's light penetrates the human spirit and exposes every motive. Be honest with God. Seek to do his will with the right intentions. Nothing is hidden from the Lord, so don't pretend that you can keep anything secret.

Jesus, help me to do the right things the right way with the right motives. Amen.

FOOD, FRIENDS, AND FAMILY

A bowl of vegetables with someone you love is better than steak with someone you hate. (Proverbs 15:17, NLT)

In the New Testament, the Bible shows that the early Christians did three things together a lot. They prayed, they told others about Jesus, and they ate meals together. When you share a meal with people, normally you do so with people you care about. When you are with people you love, it doesn't matter as much what you are eating as that you are able to be together.

Cherish the time you have with those you love because those are special memories. When your family sits down to dinner, enjoy that time to talk – no matter what you're eating. Do your part to make eating together a fun tradition with your friends and family, just as the early Christians did.

God, thank you for my friends and family and the time you give us to spend together. Amen.

LAZY FEVER

A lazy person's way is blocked with briers,
but the path of the upright is an open
highway. (Proverbs 15:19, NLT)

Pretend you are the boss of a hundred people. Fifty of those people work very hard, and the other fifty do nothing. They do not work, but instead they watch TV all day long. When it comes time to give raises, you would probably reward the hard workers and not the lazy ones. Lazy people run into troubles all the time because it takes them longer to get anything done.

In 2 Timothy, Paul wrote to the Christians that he and the other leaders were hard workers, setting an example to all the believers of hard work. Laziness and hard work are both contagious – when others see how you work they often do the same. So set the example of being an upright and hard worker.

Lord, help me to be a hard worker so that I am a good example to others. Amen.

GOD'S IDEA

The plans of the diligent lead to profit as surely as haste leads to poverty. (Proverbs 21:5, NIV)

To be hasty means to do something without thinking about it first. Gideon is a good example of someone who was not hasty. God gave him a step-by-step plan on how to defeat the Midianite army with only three hundred soldiers. Gideon and his men followed God's plan diligently, even though it didn't make sense.

By using only horns and torches, a few hundred men defeated an entire army. God's plans may not always make sense, but they are the best plans. By being patient and waiting for God to show you what to do, you will always be on the winning side.

Jesus, I want to be diligent. Show me your ways. Amen.

JOSEPH'S OBEDIENCE

*Pay attention and listen to the sayings of
the wise; apply your heart to what
I teach. (Proverbs 22:17, NIV)*

When an angel told Joseph that Herod planned on killing baby Jesus, Joseph listened. He did not wait to leave; he immediately took Mary and Jesus to Egypt just as the angel told him to do.

The Bible says that he left that night. Because Joseph listened to the Angel of the Lord and obeyed right away, he protected Jesus' life.

When you are told to clean your room right away, doing it the next day is still disobeying. God wants you to listen to him and those he placed in authority in your life – and he wants you to obey right away, not when you feel like it.

Jesus, please help me not to wait but to obey right away. Amen.

PEOPLE PERSON

Unfriendly people care only about themselves. (Proverbs 18:1, NLT)

Jesus was always spending time with people. He was often with the crowds, his disciples, or even the tax collectors. Jesus did not hide himself from everyone. At times, he did go away by himself to pray, but that was to connect with God. The rest of the time he was out with people – talking, encouraging, helping, healing.

Proverbs points out that people who are unfriendly and isolate themselves really care only about themselves. They are selfish. God does not want his people to be isolated and self-centered. Jesus was an example of how to love people by spending time with them. Don't isolate yourself. God has people he wants you to influence for him.

God, help me to remember that even when I want to be alone, I should not become isolated and selfish. Remind me that you want to use me to impact other people's lives. Amen.

DAVID AND SAUL

Before his downfall a man's heart is proud, but humility comes before honor. (Proverbs 18:12, NIV)

Few stories show how a man's pride or humility can affect his standing with God better than the story of David and Saul. Saul was Israel's king, and he became a bit prideful. Even though David had been anointed and knew he would one day be king, David was extremely humble even when Saul tried to kill him. God saw Saul's pride and David's humility. Saul was rejected as king, and David eventually took the throne in Israel.

No matter how smart you are or how good you are at sports, always be humble if you want to stay in favor of God. Pride leads to downfall, but humility comes before honor.

Jesus, I do not want to be proud and think I am better than other people. Show me how to be humble. Amen.

AVOIDING ENVY

*Don't envy sinners, but always continue
to fear the LORD. (Proverbs 23:17, NLT)*

You probably know people who do things that
are wrong. Maybe they are at school or at church
or even in your own family. You see the things
they do and you know they are wrong, yet maybe
you even feel a little jealous. But the Bible says
that you should not envy the bad things people
do. Sometimes things that may look fun end up
causing more trouble than they're worth.

If a guy at school laughs about how many
things he stole from the local store, don't let yourself desire the things he stole or the excitement
he talks about. It won't be very exciting when he
gets caught and gets punished for stealing. Sin
may seem like fun for a moment, but fearing the
Lord helps you to have a better life in the long
run.

Jesus, I know I am not perfect and that I will make mistakes, but please help me to avoid the temptation of
envying others when they do things I know are wrong.
Amen.

FEBRUARY

HUGS AND STUFF
(LOVE)

LOVE GOD FIRST

Take your son, your only son — yes, Isaac, whom you love so much — and go to the land of Moriah.
Go and sacrifice him as a burnt offering on one of the mountains, which I will show you. (Genesis 22:2, NLT)

Abraham had waited his whole life to have a child. So when God told him to take his long-awaited son that he loved so much and sacrifice him as a burnt offering, Abraham must have been both astounded and sad. But God was testing Abraham — you see, God had big plans for him, but he wanted to make sure that Abraham loved him more than anything. Jesus says in the New Testament that there is no greater commandment than to love God with all your heart, soul, mind, and strength.

God wants you to love other people, but he knows that you cannot love others fully unless you love God first and love him the most. He is like an electric outlet. By plugging into him, you are charged up and able to love others.

God, please help me to love you first and best so that I can also love others. Amen.

LOVING AND SERVING

Jacob was in love with Rachel and said, "I'll work for you seven years in return for your younger daughter Rachel." (Genesis 29:18, NIV)

Jacob loved Rachel so much that he was willing to work a whole seven years for her. He ended up working even longer than that, but can you imagine loving someone so much you would be willing to work for seven years for her? Jacob understood that when you love, you are willing to serve. You may not like a girl right now, but there is someone you love – like a parent or a friend. One way to know if you really love others is to ask yourself if you are willing to serve them or if you are only concerned with yourself.

If you do not serve or help other people out, then you are not really being loving like God wants you to. Be like Jacob – willing to serve others.

Father, please help me to live to serve others and not only myself. Amen.

LAVISH LOVE

I lavish unfailing love for a thousand generations on those who love me and obey my commands. (Exodus 20:6, NLT)

The Bible gives lots of examples of times when God shows more favor to some people than to others. God accepted Abel's offering over Cain's; he chose Jacob over Esau; he picked David to be the next king instead of Saul's son Jonathan. It is not always clear why God does what he does, but it is clear that God loves those who love him. He chose David because David was a man after God's own heart.

Be one of those people who loves God and desires to be closer to him, because God desires to be closer with you. He promises to lavish unfailing love on those who love and obey him.

Jesus, I want all of your love. Please help me to show my love for you through my actions and in my heart. Amen.

LOVE GOD ON PURPOSE

So be very careful to love the LORD your God. (Joshua 23:11, NIV)

If you love playing video games, then you probably make sure you play as often as you can. You don't just leave the video game in the corner and look at it every other month. The same is true with God. If you really love him, you shouldn't just think about him every now and then; he should be part of your life every day.

Be sure to love God on purpose. This means that you don't get lazy and forget about loving God daily. Some of the ways you can show that you love God is by reading his Word, praying and talking to him, and helping others.

Father, I want to love you on purpose. Help me not to be distracted in my circumstances, but to always keep you in mind. Amen.

LOVING YOUR FRIENDS

After David had finished talking with Saul, Jonathan became one in spirit with David, and he loved him as himself. (1 Samuel 18:1, NIV)

One of God's best gifts is friendship. You cannot choose your family, but you can choose your friends. The relationship between David and Jonathan is one of the best examples in the Bible of an awesome friendship. The main reason why is just like the verse says – Jonathan loved David as he loved himself. This meant that he wanted the best for David no matter what, even if that meant that David would become king instead of him.

God wants you to love your friends so much that you want them to do just as well – if not better – than you do. Lots of people have friends, but not everyone has a great friend like Jonathan. Be different. Be a great friend!

God, thank you for all of the friends you have placed in my life. Show me how to be a good friend and love them as you want me to love them. Amen.

GOD'S LOVE NEVER FAILS

You gave me life and showed me your unfailing love. My life was preserved by your care. (Job 10:12, NLT)

Job had everything. He had money and a big family, but more than anything he loved God. Then when he least expected it, Job lost everything. First, he lost all his wealth, then all his children were killed, and finally he got very sick. However, no matter how tough his life got, Job knew that God still loved him.

No matter what you go through in life, you can always depend on God's love. God never stops loving you, so even when things seem really bad, put a smile on your face, because the Creator of the universe is on your side. Job remembered that God was with him, loved him, and would take care of him. Even through great suffering, Job stayed faithful to God. No matter what you go through, keep loving God. He will always keep loving you.

God, thank you so much for your love even when things in my life are difficult. It is great to know I never have to worry about losing your love! Amen.

ROMANTIC LOVE

*Your love delights me, my treasure, my bride.
Your love is better than wine, your perfume more
fragrant than spices. (Song of Songs 4:10, NLT)*

Romantic love is the love between a man and a
woman. As they get older, God allows a man and
a woman to love each other to better serve him.
When Adam was first made, he was all by himself.
But God said that it was not good for man to be
alone, so he made Eve. They worked together in
the garden, and then they later had a family.

The Bible points out that two are stronger than
one, so when two people marry they are able to
serve God to an even greater degree. Girls might
not be important to you right now, but be kind to
them and treat them well. God will probably use
a girl to help you in the distant future.

Father, I pray that, as I get older, you will protect me
from girls who do not love you. I know it may be a long
way away, but please guide me to love the person you
have for me. Amen.

THE REALITY OF GOD'S LOVE

The LORD your God is with you, he is mighty to save. He will take great delight in you, he will quiet you with his love, he will rejoice over you with singing. (Zephaniah 3:17, NIV)

In case you don't already know it, God loves you. He really *really* REALLY loves you. God is not a distant God who forgets about you, is too busy for you, or just ignores you if he is in a bad mood. That never happens with God. He is always with you and always excited about you. He even sings about you! Can you imagine that? The all-powerful God gets excited about little ol' you!

Do not forget that. When other people let you down or when life gets a bit tough, remember that God loves you so much that he actually sings about you. He loves you all the time – and not just when you get an A in school or when you win the game for your soccer team. He loves you always.

Jesus, I am so excited to know that your love is real. Help me to feel and see your love. Amen.

LOVING ENEMIES

You have heard that it was said, "Love your neighbor and hate your enemy." But I tell you: Love your enemies and pray for those who persecute you, that you may be sons of your Father in heaven. (Matthew 5:43-45, NIV)

It is one thing to love your friends and your family, but it is way more difficult to love people who are mean to you. But in order to be like Jesus, you should follow his example and his teachings. He wants you to love your enemies. You may not feel like you have actual "enemies," but you probably know kids who tease you or have a family member who has hurt you. Jesus wants you to pray for them and treat them kindly.

It may seem like too much to ask, but Jesus is not asking anything from you that he did not do himself. Jesus showed love to the people who beat him up and nailed him to a cross. If Jesus can forgive people who spit at him, hit him, and killed him, you can forgive too.

God, it isn't easy to love some people at times, but please help me not to hold grudges against people. Please plant the seeds of love in my heart. Amen.

LOVING FULLY

Love the Lord your God with all your heart and with all your soul and with all your mind and with all your strength. (Mark 12:30, NIV)

How would you feel if your friends and family members only liked you a little bit? What if they didn't want to give you a hug, but instead would only shake your hand? It probably wouldn't feel very good if your friends only invited you to half of their birthday parties.

God has feelings, too. He doesn't want you to only love him a little bit. He wants you to love him because he is so excited to love you. To love him fully means to love him in your heart, in your thoughts, in your actions, and with all of your strength.

Father, I want to love you with all of my heart! You are awesome and deserve the best. Show me how to love with all my strength. Amen.

THE COST OF LOVE

*For God so loved the world that he gave his one and
only Son, that whoever believes in him shall not
perish but have eternal life. (John 3:16, NIV)*

Love is not cheap. True love came at a great cost.
God loved you and everyone you know so much
that he gave his Son so everyone would have a
chance to break free from sin and spend eternity in heaven. Ever since Adam and Eve messed
things up in the garden, people have been sinning. You, your family, and all the people you
know have sinned at some point.

The world is full of liars, thieves, and selfish
people, but God was not selfish. Even those
people who look good on the outside still have
sin in their hearts. God gave his Son so that you
could have hope for a better future. Life on earth
can be very difficult at times, but heaven will be
perfect. It is a great thing to look forward to, but
it didn't come cheap.

God, I can't imagine how much you love me! You gave
your only Son to die for me. Thank you for everything!
Amen.

LOVING LIKE JESUS

This is my commandment: Love each other in the same way I have loved you. (John 15:12, NLT)

You might hear at church that you are to love others. It sounds nice and it is the right thing to do, but you might not know how to love like you are supposed to. If you don't know or you need to be reminded about how to really love, then read about Jesus. He is the perfect example of how to love others.

Jesus forgave friends after they had said mean things. He helped and respected the elderly. He was patient with little children. He took time to spend with God alone in prayer, and he honored his mother and father. Read about Jesus in the books of Matthew, Mark, Luke and John. You'll soon discover all the ways Jesus loved. Try to do the same.

Jesus, you are my example on how to love. Help me to be more like you each and every day. Amen.

GREATEST LOVE

There is no greater love than to lay down one's life for one's friends. (John 15:13, NLT)

There is no greater love than to give your life so that others may live. Jesus did just that – and what he did set him apart from all others who have ever lived. He spoke about love. He taught others about love. But he actually lived out what he taught others. Jesus was not just a good speaker who people listened to, but he was also a light that people could follow.

Everyone needs a role model and Jesus provided that for everyone. He didn't just talk the talk, but he walked the walk. Jesus did not just tell everyone about the greatest love of all time, but he showed the greatest act of love: He laid down his life for his friends – including you.

Father, sometimes this kind of love can be scary, but you say that perfect love casts out fear, so give me your perfect love. Amen.

WORKS OF LOVE

If I give all I possess to the poor and surrender my body to the flames, but have not love, I gain nothing. (1 Corinthians 13:3, NIV)

Some people try to make up for all of their bad mistakes by doing good works. However, the Bible shows that this is not the answer. God does want you to do the right things in your actions, but actions alone cannot save you. God wants you to do the right things in love.

He says in this verse that you could give all of your money to the poor and even die for them, but if you do not love those you were helping, then you gain nothing at all. God does not want his people just to be robots and only do what they are supposed to because they don't have any choice. He would rather have them do the right thing because of his love working through them.

God, I know that I need to be loving even when I do good things. You want me to love others no matter what I do, so please show me how to do that! Amen.

LOVE IS KIND

Love is patient and kind. (1 Corinthians 13:4, NLT)

Do you get upset when other people make small mistakes? Do you say mean things to a kid at school who has braces and glasses? If you do, then you are not living in love. Love is patient, which means that if you love people with God's kind of love you don't get upset when they mess up or when they are not as quick to get something done.

Love is also kind, which means you are nice to the person other people make fun of, you reach out to the new kid, you help out when others might laugh at you.

Patience and kindness. See if you can practice being patient and kind to people today.

Father, sometimes I want what I want right now, so please help me to be patient. Show me how to be kind to others around me – people I might not even notice. Amen.

LOVE IS NOT JEALOUS

*Love is not jealous or boastful or proud
or rude. (1 Corinthians 13:4-5, NLT)*

When good things happen to other people, you should not be jealous. Jealousy is getting upset that someone else got what you did not. So if a friend got the bike you wanted, it is not okay to get angry about it. God does not want you to worry about what other people have. On the other side, however, God also does not want you to be boastful or proud about what you have.

If you got a new bike, you might want to show it to your friends, but you don't want to brag and be boastful. That would be rude, and that's another thing that love is not. Instead, when you have God's kind of love, you are happy for others, humble about what you have, and gracious. Since Jesus was the perfect example of love and you as a Christian are to be Christlike, then learn to love as he wants you to love.

Jesus, you were not jealous or proud or rude. Help me to be more like you. Amen.

LOVE ISN'T DEMANDING

[Love] does not demand its own way.
(1 Corinthians 13:5, NLT)

One of the biggest problems people have with bullies is that they are pushy. They demand their own way. They take other people's food and money without even caring about the people they push around. Bullies do not live through love. The Bible says love does not demand its own way; it is not pushy. Love does not try to force others to do something they don't want to do.

God wants you to be the anti-bully. This means that you should be the opposite of pushy. This doesn't mean that you never take a stand for what is right, but rather you realize that you shouldn't be demanding or pushy. Love means not demanding your own way, but instead being aware of others' needs and desires.

Jesus, help me not to always demand my way. I know that is not the right thing to do. Show me when I need to be aware of other people's needs and desires. Amen.

LOVE ISN'T GROUCHY

[Love] is not irritable. (1 Corinthians 13:5, NLT)

When you are tired or if you have a stomach ache, it can be hard sometimes not to be grumpy. God wants you not to be grumpy when things get you down, but to still be an example of love to others. That can be hard sometimes. After all, how can you love when you just don't feel good or when you're frustrated?

Jesus gave you an example. He was often faced with difficulty – crowds of people making demands, religious leaders asking questions, people following him, constant teaching and healing. But Jesus didn't get grumpy or grouchy or irritable. He loved God and he knew he was doing what God wanted him to do.

So the next time you feel grumpy, ask God to help you show love instead. In fact, when you are loving toward people when they expect you to be grouchy, it shows them even more clearly how much Jesus means to you.

I can get grumpy sometimes, but I don't want to be like that. Change my heart, Lord. Amen.

LOVE DOESN'T KEEP TRACK

[Love] keeps no record of being wronged.
(1 Corinthians 13:5, NLT)

You probably have made some mistakes in the past. Maybe you forgot to clean your room, or you got a bad grade in math, or you said something you shouldn't have. If you have made mistakes, don't worry – everyone messes up at some point. However, it wouldn't be fun if your parents reminded you every day of every mistake you ever made. It wouldn't feel good if you were taking out the trash and they reminded you about the one time you didn't take it out. It wouldn't feel good, would it?

This is why God says that love does not keep a record of wrongs. This means that you shouldn't always bring up all the mistakes other people have made. You wouldn't like it and neither would they. Don't keep track of the times people have wronged you. Forgive as God has forgiven you.

Jesus, help me to forgive those who have hurt me. Amen.

LOVE LIKES TRUTH

*[Love] does not rejoice about injustice
but rejoices whenever the truth
wins out. (1 Corinthians 13:6, NLT)*

If Ben and Tim got into a fight and you knew that Tim started it, then it wouldn't be acting in love to lie and blame Ben for starting it so that Tim wouldn't get into trouble. Even if Tim is your friend, true love desires truth and justice.

God is a God of love, but he also is a just God. If God rejoices when truth wins out, then every time you lie or are on the side of injustice, you place yourself on the opposite team of God. You want to be on God's side, so always cheer for truth, tell the truth, and love the truth.

God, help me to love truth like you love truth. Amen.

LOVE DOESN'T GIVE UP

*Love never gives up, never loses faith,
is always hopeful, and endures through every
circumstance. (1 Corinthians 13:7, NLT)*

If you cheer for a sports team and really love that team, then you hope that eventually they will win the championship. Even if your team has a tough season, even if they don't win, you look forward to next year.

Some fans give up on their teams when they don't play well, but that is not true love. When you love someone or something, you should not just love it when it benefits you, but you should love in the tough times, too.

God's love is much greater than just a love for a game. God loves you in your worst times. His kind of love shows you how you should love when others have tough times, too.

God, I don't want to be a quitter. Fill me with true love that is always hopeful. Amen.

LOVE LASTS

Love will last forever! (1 Corinthians 13:8, NLT)

Sometimes people we know move away, others die, and sometimes things we like get broken or ruined. But not love. Love doesn't disappear. God's love is always present and will always be present even when you get to heaven. His love can never move away or die or get ruined. It lasts forever.

Maybe you don't have the perfect family and perhaps you don't feel loved sometimes. You need to know this ... *you are loved*. God loves you and his love will last forever. Sometimes when you feel loved the least is the most important time for you to love others. Give people you know a hug and tell them how much God loves them. Love will last forever, so stay in practice by continuing to love.

God, I know I am young, but please help me to truly realize how important it is to live in love. Amen.

EVEN WHEN OTHERS DON'T CARE

So I will very gladly spend for you everything I have and expend myself as well. If I love you more, will you love me less? (2 Corinthians 12:15, NIV)

Brad got a new puppy and he loved his pet so much. He fed it and took it for walks, but one day as the dog got bigger, it ran away. Brad never saw him again, and he was heartbroken. When you love someone, it does not always mean that person will love you back. God loves the whole world, and yet lots of people reject him because they want to do their own thing.

This is why you should not love others just so they will love you in return. If you love others just to get something back, then you will often be disappointed. But if you love others just because God loves you, then you will be blessed by God. Love others even when they don't seem to care. You never know what kind of difference your love might make in their lives.

Sometimes it can be discouraging when nothing I do seems to make a difference, but help me to love and do the right thing no matter what. Amen.

LOVE YOURSELF

The entire law is summed up in a single command: "Love your neighbor as yourself." (Galatians 5:14, NIV)

God wants you to love other people, but he doesn't want you to love them just a little bit. He wants you to love them as much as you love yourself. In order to love others as much as you love yourself, you need to first love yourself.

But what does that mean? It does not mean that you become arrogant or think you are the best at everything. Instead, loving yourself means that you recognize that you are special in God's eyes. You are not junk. You are valuable to him. When you know that you are special, you can love yourself and love other people because they are special, too.

Jesus, help me to love myself so that I can love others. Amen.

FRUIT AND LOVE

The fruit of the Spirit is love. (Galatians 5:22, NIV)

Do you have the Holy Spirit working in you? The way you know is if you have the fruit of the Spirit growing in your life. Galatians 5:22-23 lists several kinds of "fruit" that should be blossoming in the lives of people who love Jesus. Fruit is something that other people can see in your life just by looking.

The first fruit on the list is love. When you walk in love, you show people that you have God's Holy Spirit working in you. God could have chosen any of the other fruits to start with, but he didn't. He chose love to be listed first. You see, love is the basis for the other fruits of the Spirit. You cannot have joy, peace, patience, kindness, goodness, faithfulness, gentleness, or self-control without first having love. If you want to be full of the Holy Spirit then LOVE!

God, please help me to be growing the fruit of the Spirit in my life. Let the Holy Spirit start with love. Amen.

LOVE AND MERCY

Be completely humble and gentle;
be patient, bearing with one another
in love. (Ephesians 4:2, NIV)

Your friends are going to annoy you sometimes; your family might drive you crazy from time to time. But God wants you to be patient. He wants you to show grace to others. Everyone makes mistakes, so don't be so tough on them. God also points out that you should be humble and gentle because you, too, will make mistakes.

You are not perfect either, and your friends and family members will sometimes need to show patience to you as well. When you love people by being patient when they make mistakes, they often are willing to show you more mercy and tolerance when you mess up. After all, God is patient with you every day!

God, help me to be patient with others. Remind me that I often need people to be patient with me. Teach me to be humble and gentle. Amen.

KEEP LOVING

I pray that your love will overflow more and more, and that you will keep on growing in knowledge and understanding. (Philippians 1:9, NLT)

You might be good at loving other people. Perhaps you are kind to your parents and friendly to the boy that others pick on at school. Maybe you give your allowance to those who have less money and food than you do. But there is always room for you to grow. Even if you already love a lot, you can still love more.

Jesus' love is bottomless, which means it goes on and on forever; it can never run out. Paul prayed that the love of the believers would overflow more and more. Ask God to give you so much love for others that it overflows.

God, grow my love more and more and more so that it overflows onto others. Amen.

CHRISTIAN LOVE

Greet all the brothers and sisters with
Christian love. (1 Thessalonians 5:26, NLT)

The Bible says to love other Christians, so when you meet other people who are Christians, do not see them as strangers. Instead, they are actually your brothers and sisters in the Lord. Christianity is one big family. This means that you have family members who live in other parts of America, Europe, Asia, and Africa – maybe even in Antarctica!

God's family is big. Be excited that you are a part of something that is much bigger than you. God's family was started a long time before you were born and will likely go on after you grow old. Love other Christians like you would love your own family. After all, one day you'll live with them forever in heaven!

Lord, I want to show other Christians a special love. Show me how to do that, God. Amen.

LOVE HURTS

Then Jesus wept. (John 11:35, NLT)

John 11:35 is the shortest Scripture in the Bible, but it shows how much Jesus loves those he cares about. When he heard that his friend Lazarus had died he cried. Jesus loved his friend just like he loves you. He feels the pain you go through each and every time you hurt.

When you love, it opens yourself to feeling how other people feel, because you begin to care about them. If you have ever been sad because one of your parents or siblings cried then you know what it is like to love someone so much that you feel their pain. God gives you that ability so you can help love on and pray for those who hurt.

Jesus, help me to love people even when it might not feel good. Fill me with your love so I can love like you. Amen.

MARCH

THE ROAD MAP (THE POWER OF THE BIBLE)

THE POWER TO LIVE

Jesus told him, "No! The Scriptures say, 'People do not live by bread alone, but by every word that comes from the mouth of God.'" (Matthew 4:4, NLT)

There are certain things every person needs to be able to live. Everyone needs water, oxygen, and food, but Jesus says that you need more than just the basics to live. He points out that you also need the word of God. The Bible is God's word.

It is his voice to you telling you how to live and what he is like. The Bible is full of wise answers to the big questions everyone has – like how people were made, why evil exists, and what happens when people die. Food and water are important for your physical life, but the Bible is even more important. It helps your spirit to live. It has the words that give eternal life.

Jesus, help me to live on the word of God. I want it to give me strength and guide me. Amen.

POWER THAT DRAWS PEOPLE

One day as Jesus was preaching on the shore of the Sea of Galilee, great crowds pressed in on him to listen to the word of God. (Luke 5:1, NLT)

If you hold a magnet next to a metal pole, the magnet will stick to the pole. Magnetism is a powerful force – the stronger the magnet, the stronger the pull. God is a powerful magnet because he is a powerful force. People pressed in around Jesus because they were drawn to him. He taught them Scripture and truth, and people from all over the place came to hear him preach.

They were like pieces of metal drawn to a magnet. In the same way, God's word draws people because it is truth, and people long to know the truth. When you read God's word and start to understand and live it, people will be drawn to you, too. Point them to God and his word. Help them find the truth they're looking for.

God, thank you so much for your mighty word. Please draw even more people to your word so they may know the truth. Amen.

OBEY GOD'S WORD

[Jesus] replied, "Blessed rather are those who hear the word of God and obey it." (Luke 11:28, NIV)

If your mom told you to clean your room, she would be upset if you ignored her. If you had your headphones on so that you couldn't hear her, it might bug her a little bit but she might understand. However, if you *did* hear her and you *still* didn't clean your room, then she would likely be more upset, because you directly disobeyed her.

In the same way, God wants you to listen to his word, but he also wants you to obey it. Those who do obey are blessed. Those who do not obey are not blessed. So be blessed by obeying the word of God.

Father, I want to not just read your word, I want to live it! Amen.

NOT ALWAYS POPULAR

*When some ... learned that Paul was preaching
the word of God in Berea, they went there
and stirred up trouble. (Acts 17:13, NLT)*

The word of God will attract many people, but it will anger others. Some people don't want to listen to anyone – least of all to God. These kinds of people like to cause trouble. They don't want other people to hear the words of God, so they do what they can to stop those who are preaching and teaching.

This is not a new thing. Many people don't want to think about God or know that he has plans and laws for them; they would rather go their own way. But nothing can stop the truth of God's word. God will make sure that those who want to hear his message will get the chance. And maybe you'll get to be the one to share it!

God, please open the hearts of those who don't know you. Soften them and let your words of wisdom minister to them. Amen.

A TREASURE

Now I entrust you to God and the message of his grace that is able to build you up and give you an inheritance with all those he has set apart for himself. (Acts 20:32, NLT)

The Bible is not just a book – it is a treasure. It is more valuable than gold, diamonds, or a million dollars. All of those things can disappear, but the treasures in the Bible can never be taken away. When you believe the truth in the Bible about God and Jesus, then you become a part of God's family. God has big plans for your life on earth and for your life in heaven.

You learn about those plans in the Bible. That's what makes this book a treasure! It builds you up and gives you great promises for the future. You may not be rich on earth, but your heavenly Father is very wealthy and he has an inheritance set apart for you – and it will be better than anything you can imagine!

Thank you, God, for this wonderful treasure that tells me more about you, your ways, and your awesome promises to me. Amen.

THE TRUTH

*We do not use deception, nor do we distort
the word of God. (2 Corinthians 4:2, NIV)*

The Bible is the source of all truth. It is God's words on what to do and what not to do. It is a letter to you and all humanity of how much God loves you and what he expects from those he loves. But there are some people who try to make the Bible say things that are not true. They try to get people to agree with them for bad reasons.

God will judge people who make things up about the Bible that aren't true, so it is important that you only speak the truth about the Bible. How can you know? Be sure to listen carefully in church, read the Bible carefully for yourself, and ask questions of people who know more than you. As you learn the truth that is in the Bible, you will be able to recognize and reject anything that is not true.

God, help me to understand the Bible and show me how to tell others about it in an honest and truthful way. Amen.

A WEAPON

Put on salvation as your helmet, and take the sword of the Spirit, which is the word of God. (Ephesians 6:17, NLT)

You are a warrior. If you believe that Jesus is Lord and you have accepted him as your personal Savior, then you are one of God's warriors in the battle against Satan. This does not mean you carry a gun, but you do have a weapon. This weapon is different than most – it's called the "sword of the Spirit." Your weapon is the Bible. When you read the Bible, it shows you how to live, tells you promises, and gives you the words to pray.

The Bible is the truth, so when you read and pray its words, you are praying the promises of God out loud and speaking the truth against the enemy. Like a sword in the hand of a mighty warrior, the truth beats back Satan, your enemy. The Bible is powerful, so read as much as you can!

Lord, I want to be a warrior for you. Not one who hurts people, but a warrior who uses the sword of the Spirit to stand up for truth. Amen.

NOT CHAINED

*This is my gospel, for which I am suffering
even to the point of being chained like a criminal.
But God's word is not chained. (2 Timothy 2:8-9, NIV)*

Jesus was arrested and then killed on a cross. Paul preached in lots of different cities, but he too was arrested. In fact, lots of Christians in the Bible and across the centuries have been arrested and even killed because of their belief in Jesus as Lord.

Bad people have tried to stop the word of God from being preached, but nothing they have done has worked. Like 2 Timothy says, even though people can be chained and put in jail, nothing can ever stop the word of God. The Bible cannot be chained; it is too strong. The Bible is powerful because it is true. Nothing can stop God's truth.

God, I feel safe knowing that your word is stronger than anything else on the planet. Amen.

LIVING, ACTIVE, SHARP

For the word of God is living and active. Sharper than any double-edged sword, it penetrates even to dividing soul and spirit, joints and marrow; it judges the thoughts and attitudes of the heart. (Hebrews 4:12, NIV)

The word of God is living and active – but what does that mean? How can a book be alive? The words in the Bible "speak" to people all the time. People all over the world read God's word and God speaks to them about their particular situation or need. When you open the Bible, God speaks to you in the stories, the psalms, the life and words of Jesus, and the letters. God helps you know how to handle a situation, the right words to say, or how to help a friend. Sometimes the words in the Bible "penetrate" your heart, meaning that they speak to you about an attitude or action God wants you to change.

So read God's Word every day and let God speak to you through it.

God, I know I am not perfect, but let your holy word shine on my life and show me where I can grow. Amen.

ROAD MAP OF LIFE

"The time has come," he said. "The kingdom of God is near. Repent and believe the good news!" (Mark 1:15, NIV)

If you went camping and got lost, it would be scary with the large trees that block your view and the fear of wild animals. If you had a map, however, you could see which direction you needed to go to find your campsite. Real life can be scary, too. There are some people who are scarier than wild animals, and it's easy to feel lost at times.

The good news is that God gave you a map to help you in life. It shows you what kinds of people to hang out with, how to treat your parents, and how much God loves you. The Bible is the map of life. God made it for you to help you see where you need to go.

Please show me how to live, God. Show me what paths to take and which paths to avoid. Amen.

NOT ALWAYS ACCEPTED

Not all the Israelites accepted the good news.
For Isaiah says, "Lord, who has believed
our message?" (Romans 10:16, NIV)

Justin walked into the classroom and told everyone that free ice cream, chocolate, and pizza were being given away in the lunch room. But no one believed him, so nobody went to the lunch room for the treats. Problem was, Justin was telling the truth!

Sometimes people have a tough time believing something that seems too good to be true. Jesus told people about heaven and God's promises, but many did not believe him because it sounded too good to be true. You may tell others about God and his offer of salvation, but they might not believe you. This is not your fault. All you can do is tell others what you have learned. The rest is in God's hands.

God, I do not understand why people would reject your free gift of love, but I pray that you can help them see the truth and love you offer. Amen.

WHERE THE ANSWERS ARE

[Jesus] added, "Now go and learn the meaning of this Scripture: 'I want you to show mercy, not offer sacrifices.' For I have come to call not those who think they are righteous, but those who know they are sinners." (Matthew 9:13, NLT)

When you take a test in school, do you ever get nervous that you'll get a bad grade? If you know what to study, it's not as scary because at least you know what the test will be about.

God is not a mean teacher. He gives you the important answers you need to know. All you have to do is look for them – and the answers are in God's word. So, if you are afraid that you will mess up in life, take a deep breath. All you have to do is read and obey what God asks you to do in the Bible.

Father, I know that I am not good enough and cannot earn your love, but I am so excited that you give your love freely to me. Amen.

SPEAKS OF THE FUTURE

"Rather than tearing it apart, let's throw dice for it. This fulfilled the Scripture that says, "They divided my garments among themselves and threw dice for my clothing." So that is what they did. (John 19:24, NLT)

You probably already know that Jesus came to earth to die for your sins, so you could be reunited with God and spend eternity in heaven. What you might not know is that all that happened to Jesus was foreseen years before it happened.

"Foreseen" means that people knew the future before it happened; many of the prophets in the Old Testament talked about the coming of the Messiah. For instance, David foresaw the events in the verse above when he wrote in a psalm, "They divide my garments among them and cast lots for my clothing" (Psalm 22:18, NIV).

God knows everything. He knows the beginning and the end. So be confident in the Bible. It is the truth – now and forever.

Lord, thank you for knowing what will happen and having a good plan for me. Amen.

INSPIRED BY GOD

All Scripture is inspired by God and is useful to teach us what is true and to make us realize what is wrong in our lives. It corrects us when we are wrong and teaches us to do what is right. (2 Timothy 3:16, NLT)

God wrote the Bible. He inspired Moses, the prophets, Paul, and many of Jesus' followers to write down God's messages for people and to tell about all of the things God did for them. Their words help you to know what happened and to have a better understanding of God's power, love, and wisdom. God inspired the writers of the Bible to say what he wanted them to say. So you can trust that the Bible's words are true and can help you understand what is wrong in your life.

The entire Bible is inspired by God. Enjoy your favorite parts, but don't stop there. God has important things to say to you all the way through his word. The more you read, the more God will guide you, and help you do what is right.

Jesus, I can walk boldly in the things the Bible says because it is inspired by you. Amen.

OF GOD, NOT MAN

Above all, you must understand that no prophecy of Scripture came about by the prophet's own interpretation. (2 Peter 1:20, NIV)

In the Bible, God spoke to his people through prophets. These prophets gave messages to the people – sometimes they helped the people see what they were doing wrong; sometimes they told the people what they needed to do; other times they foretold the future. However, the prophets never did all of that on their own – God gave them that ability and they always told the people that their messages where from the Lord.

In the same way, God has given you some kind of talent or gift. Maybe you are good in school, or maybe you can sing. It is important for you to remember that no matter how good you are at something, that gift came from God. You should always give him the credit.

Jesus, I know that the things I can do well came not from myself, but are gifts from you. You are awesome! Amen.

THE BIBLE PROVES TRUE

Every word of God proves true. He is a shield to all who come to him for protection. (Proverbs 30:5, NLT)

In the movie, *The Incredibles*, the daughter Violet has a super power where she can put a force field around her to protect herself. You also have a super power. God says he is a shield for all those who trust him. Because "every word of God proves true," you can trust that this promise of God's shield that will protect you is also true.

You can depend on God to protect you no matter what. That doesn't mean you won't ever get hurt or have difficult times. Sometimes God works through those difficult times to make you better and stronger. His plans may be different than yours, but you can always trust them. God is your shield. Trust him.

You are so dependable. Even when others let me down you are always there for me! Amen.

THE BIBLE LASTS FOREVER

The grass withers and the flowers fade, but the word of our God stands forever. (Isaiah 40:8, NLT)

God's word will last forever. The Bible was written thousands of years ago and lots of people have tried to get rid of it for a long time. Yet it remains the most popular book in the world. The Bible will never fade away, never be lost, never disappear.

Even though generations pass and people die, even though flowers fade and time keeps going by, God's word outlasts them all. This is God's plan. His word will last forever, so you and everyone else can know God's heart.

The Bible you read today has the same message as it has had for people across the centuries. God and his message never change.

Forever is a very long time. I don't fully understand it, but it is exciting to know that you outlast anything and everyone. Amen.

ONE DAY IT WILL BE CLEAR

After he was raised from the dead, his disciples recalled what he had said. Then they believed the Scripture and the words that Jesus had spoken. (John 2:22, NIV)

Jesus taught a lot of things to his disciples. One of the things he told them was that he would die and be raised from the dead. For some reason they didn't understand what Jesus had told them until after it had all happened. Even though the Scripture the disciples knew (what we call our Old Testament) also taught that the Messiah would die and rise again, they didn't understand.

When you read the Bible, you might not understand some things until after you get a bit older. But you should still try to learn as much as you can because, like the disciples, one day you will understand. One day, some of the things in the Bible that you don't understand now will make perfect sense. God will give you the messages you need right when you need them.

God, I know you will do things that I don't understand, but help me to understand more and more as I grow up. Amen.

BLESSINGS TO THOSE WHO BELIEVE

Anyone who believes in me may come and drink! For the Scriptures declare, "Rivers of living water will flow from his heart." (John 7:38, NLT)

The Bible says that if someone has faith the size of a mustard seed, then that person can move mountains. You may be young, but if you have faith in God and what he says in Scripture, then God can work through you.

It doesn't matter if you are short, weak, or have asthma or some other problem. When you have faith in God, rivers of living water will pour out of your heart. "Living water" pictures refreshment and cleansing. With God in your heart, you will send out refreshment to everyone around you, like a river of clean water. You might just be a blessing to everyone around you!

God, bless me as I read your word. I want your river of life to run through me. Amen.

FREEDOM FROM SIN

The Scriptures declare that we are all prisoners of sin, so we receive God's promise of freedom only by believing in Jesus Christ. (Galatians 3:22, NLT)

Before Jesus died on the cross, everyone was a prisoner of sin because sin separated every person from God. Jesus' death offered you and everyone else a new promise – the promise of freedom from being imprisoned to sin. This is what the Bible calls the good news. It is good news because anyone who asks for forgiveness is forgiven.

Those who believe in Jesus are set free from sin. That doesn't mean you won't sin anymore, but it does mean that you have the Holy Spirit in you to help you try not to sin and to do what is right. We get that freedom only by believing in Jesus. No wonder it's called good news!

Jesus, thank you for setting me free from sin. Thanks for helping me every day to live for you! Amen.

PAY ATTENTION

*Until I get there, focus on reading the Scriptures
to the church, encouraging the believers,
and teaching them. (1 Timothy 4:13, NLT)*

The Bible is a very big book, and some parts you might not understand for a while. However, the Bible is the voice of God. The very reading of it helps and encourages those who hear its words. God does not want you to only read the Bible by yourself, he also wants it to be read aloud to many people, like at church.

You should listen quietly in church when the Bible is being read out loud and when the minister is preaching. Paul told Timothy, who was a pastor, to read the Bible, and then to encourage and teach the people. The minister studies the Bible and brings a message to your church every Sunday. So listen carefully in church. Follow along while the Bible is being read, and pay attention to those who teach you.

God, thank you for my church and for the preachers and teachers who study your word and teach it. Help me to pay attention. Amen.

ULTIMATE TEACHER

All Scripture is inspired by God and is useful to teach us what is true and to make us realize what is wrong in our lives. It corrects us when we are wrong and teaches us to do what is right. (2 Timothy 3:16, NLT)

School is important. In school you learn about reading, writing, math, and other things. The reason you go to school is to learn as much as you can to train and prepare you for life.

Did you know that hundreds of years ago, children in school used to learn to read by reading the Bible? The teachers understood that the best teacher is the Bible – not just for reading, of course, but for learning how to live. Nowadays most schools don't teach the Bible, so you need to take the time to learn it on your own and at church.

Learn as much as you can about the Bible because, as important as all of your schooling is, learning God's word is even more important for a successful life.

Teach me everything you want me to know. I am hungry to know as much as I can. Amen.

WORSHIP ONLY GOD

*You must not have any other god
but me. (Exodus 20:3, NLT)*

The Bible is full of good things for you to know. One of the first lessons God gave to his children, the nation of Israel, was the Ten Commandments. These were ten basic laws for everyone to obey.

The first of these commandments was not to worship any other god. God does not share worship with anyone or anything. This means that when you worship the God of the Bible, you don't obey laws of another religion. It also means not to make a sports player or movie star or money more important to you than God.

Keep God first in all that you do.

God, you are the only true God. I give you my worship and my love. Amen.

NO IDOLS

*You must not make for yourself an idol of any
kind or an image of anything in the heavens
or on the earth or in the sea. (Exodus 20:4, NLT)*

Sometimes people want to talk to God so much that they make statues that look like animals and they call them "gods." One example in the Bible is when the Israelites made a golden calf so people could worship it. They began to believe that the statue they made was really their God. This may sound funny to you, but people really do worship statues made of wood or stone and think they are their gods. These statues are called "idols" and their worship is called "idolatry."

Since God is so big and awesome, he doesn't want you to worship something that is so tiny compared to him. God is not a statue. God has said you can talk directly to him – so why would you talk to anything else?

Father, no idol could capture how amazing you are. I will worship and talk to only you. Amen.

RESPECT GOD'S NAME

You shall not misuse the name of the LORD your God, for the LORD will not hold anyone guiltless who misuses his name. (Exodus 20:7, NIV)

In most countries, kids do not call adults by their first names. The reason is that it is a sign of respect to call them by their title. In school or with your friends' parents, you call those adults "Mr." or "Mrs." instead of using their first names.

In the same way, God says not to misuse his name because it is a sign of disrespect to him. Be sure to only use God's name when you worship, pray or when you are talking to others about him. Many people say his name just as an expression when they're surprised or angry, but that is disrespectful of God. Don't say his name out of anger or simply to joke around. Respect God and respect his name.

Lord, I honor and respect your name. Jesus, Jesus, Jesus, I love you and thank you. Amen.

GOD'S DAY

*Remember to observe the Sabbath day
by keeping it holy. (Exodus 20:8, NLT)*

After God created the world and everything in it, the Bible says that on the seventh day, God rested. In the Ten Commandments, God tells his people to keep the seventh day, the Sabbath, holy. God knew that people would begin to work hard and forget to rest and worship him, so he assigned a special day each week that people should set aside for rest and worship.

It might be easy to get so busy that you forget to go to church, but God wants you to show he is important to you. You can keep the Sabbath day holy by going to church and worshiping God.

Lord, teach me how to keep the Sabbath holy in a way that is pleasing to you. Amen.

HONOR YOUR PARENTS

*Honor your father and mother. Then you will live a long, full life in the land the L*ORD *your God is giving you. (Exodus 20:12, NLT)*

God wants you to honor your parents. To "honor" means to show respect and listen to what they say. God has placed them over your life, so show them the kind of respect and love you would to God himself. Your parents are human, so they will make mistakes from time to time, but you should still honor them. In fact, you honor God by honoring your parents, and you dishonor God when you dishonor your parents.

It is so important that, in this commandment, God says to honor your mom and dad if you want a long life. God says this to show that he is serious about this commandment.

God, I will honor my parents even when they make mistakes, because I am honoring you when I do. Amen.

DON'T KILL

You must not murder. (Exodus 20:13, NLT)

You probably have never even thought about murdering someone, but you probably have seen a lot of fake murders on television, in movies, and in video games. While it might seem like fun to kill people in your video game, it is important to understand that violence is not harmless or fun or exciting. Murder is one of the worst sins a person can do because it takes away one of God's greatest gifts – it takes away life. Violence is a crime against God, and whoever is involved in violence will be punished.

Sometimes people get very angry and they hurt other people. Real murders happen every day – you hear about them in the news. You should pray for those who are in pain and then try to hurt others. Hurting God's children hurts God.

Lord, please change the hearts of those people who want to harm others. Please show them the mistakes they are making. Amen.

DON'T BE JEALOUS

*You must not commit adultery. You must not
covet your neighbor's house. You must not covet
your neighbor's wife, male or female servant,
ox or donkey, or anything else that belongs
to your neighbor. (Exodus 20:14, 17, NLT)*

To "covet" means to want something that someone else has – so much so that you get jealous.
(The command to "not commit adultery" refers to
married people not wanting someone else's husband or wife.) Both of these commandments tell
people to be thankful for what they have.

Sometimes people get so jealous that it's all
they can think about. Their jealousy makes them
really sad and angry. Obviously, that is not how
God wants his people to live. You might get a little
jealous because some of your friends have nicer
bikes, better clothes, and live in bigger homes,
but God wants you to be thankful for what you
do have. Don't worry about what other people
have.

Lord, help me to be happy with what I have and not
worry about what I do not have. Amen.

DON'T STEAL

You must not steal. (Exodus 20:15, NLT)

Do not steal. This is something you probably already know. It is not right to take something that isn't yours. Stealing means you are coveting someone else's possessions. Coveting means to desire or really want what someone else has. If you steal, you are breaking two commandments at the same time. You want what someone else has (coveting), then you take it for yourself (stealing). You might know people who take things from stores or from other people, thinking that it really doesn't matter. But it does. Stealing breaks God's laws.

If you try to do good all by yourself it might be tough, but when you look to Jesus for help then it becomes easier. Jesus wants you to be content with what you have. Trust God to help you make the right decisions by praying and trusting that he will take care of you.

God, I do not want to steal, so please keep me from any temptation. Help me to be trustworthy. Amen.

DO NOT LIE

You must not testify falsely against your neighbor. (Exodus 20:16, NLT)

Pinocchio is one of the most famous examples of someone who lied. Every time he lied, his nose grew. If that really happened, there would be lots of people walking around with really long noses! Sometimes people do not take lying seriously. However, God takes lying so seriously that he put it in the Ten Commandments, right next to stealing and killing.

The reason why God does not like lying is because God loves truth. When you lie, you are not speaking truth, so you violate one of God's greatest loves. The words "testify falsely against your neighbor" refers to lying about others, which causes great trouble for them.

Show God you love him by loving what he loves. You should start by loving to tell the truth and refusing to lie.

Jesus, may my lips speak only truth. Please help me to be wise by not lying about and to other people. Amen.

APRIL

WHAT NOT TO DO: EXAMPLES FROM THE BIBLE

THE SNAKE – DOUBTING GOD

Now the serpent was more crafty than any of the wild animals the Lord God had made. He said to the woman, "Did God really say, 'You must not eat from any tree in the garden'?" (Genesis 3:1, NIV)

In the Garden of Eden, everything was perfect. There was no crime, no hunger, and no crying. But then the serpent came and talked Adam and Eve into breaking the one rule that God gave them. The serpent did this by questioning God and putting doubt about God's goodness into Eve's mind.

Adam and Even sinned, and suddenly their perfect world was no longer perfect at all. The devil's tactics have never really changed. He will try to place doubt in your mind about God, but don't be like Adam and Eve. Trust God and his goodness no matter what.

God, help me not to listen to anyone who would cause me to question you and your love for me. Amen.

HAMAN — UNFORGIVENESS

Haman, realizing that the king had already decided his fate, stayed behind to beg Queen Esther for his life. (Esther 7:7, NIV)

Haman became a very powerful leader, but a man named Mordecai didn't show him the type of respect he felt he deserved. Haman wanted Mordecai to bow to him, but Mordecai wouldn't because he was a Jew and would bow only to God. Haman became very angry, so he planned to kill Mordecai and all of the Jews along with him. Queen Esther, who happened to be a relative of Mordecai and also a Jew, loved the Lord. She bravely convinced the king that Haman was the problem, not Mordecai. The king agreed and he punished Haman with death.

Haman should never have let his anger become a plan for murder. When someone hurts you or makes you mad, staying mad and refusing to forgive ends up hurting you. It's much better to forgive and let it go.

God, sometimes I don't want to forgive, but I know I should. I need your help! Amen.

JOSEPH'S BROTHERS — JEALOUSY

Jacob loved Joseph more than any of his other children. So one day Jacob had a special gift made for Joseph – a beautiful robe. But his brothers hated Joseph because their father loved him more than the rest of them. (Genesis 37:3-4, NLT)

Joseph's dad loved him so much that he gave him a coat of many different colors. Such a colorful and beautiful garment was very rare back in biblical times. And, as you can imagine, this made Joseph's brothers very jealous. This would be like if your parents bought your brother a brand-new bike but didn't get you anything. On top of this, Joseph was having lots of dreams about his brothers bowing to him. Finally, the brothers got so jealous that they thought about killing Joseph. But instead, they sold him into slavery.

Don't allow yourself to be like Joseph's brothers, because jealousy can cause you to resent people and even do dumb things. God wants you to be happy with what you have.

God, help me to be happy with what I have. Help me not to be jealous of others. Amen.

GOLIATH — PRIDE

Goliath stood and shouted a taunt across to the Israelites. "Why are you all coming out to fight?" he called. "I am the Philistine champion, but you are only the servants of Saul. Choose one man to come down here and fight me!" (1 Samuel 17:8, NLT)

Goliath was huge! He was over nine feet tall. That is bigger than anybody alive today. He thought he could beat anybody. Because of his pride, he taunted God's army. The Bible says that pride comes before a fall, which means that anyone who is prideful will be humbled.

Goliath was humbled. He not only got beat, but he got beat by a kid who had no weapons but a few stones. Pride means that you think you're better than anyone else, and no one likes people who act that way.

God wants you to be humble, which means thanking him for the things that you can do well, appreciating others, and being kind.

Lord, I don't want to be prideful like Goliath. Instead, help me to be humble. Amen.

SAUL – TURNING FROM GOD

Saul then said to his advisers, "Find a woman who is a medium, so I can go and ask her what to do." His advisers replied, "There is a medium at Endor." Then he went to the woman's home at night. (1 Samuel 28:7-8, NLT)

Saul was originally a good guy. God had chosen him to be king, but then he started to turn away from God. When God began to show favor to David, Saul tried several times to kill David. In the end, Saul had turned so far away from God that he even went to talk to a witch (called a medium) for guidance.

You might have obeyed God when you were younger and even now you might do what's right, but as you get older don't become like Saul. Some people think as they grow up that they know more than God does, but they don't. Stay close to God and he will stay close to you.

Jesus, help me to always listen to you, so that I don't become like Saul. Amen.

PHARAOH – REFUSING TO LISTEN

Pharaoh said, "Who is the LORD, that I should obey him and let Israel go? I do not know the LORD and I will not let Israel go." (Exodus 5:2, NIV)

Moses went to Pharaoh with God's message to free the Israelites from slavery, but Pharaoh refused to listen. He probably thought that he was more powerful than the God of a bunch of people who were slaves – obviously their God couldn't be very powerful or they wouldn't be slaves.

But even though God showed his power through many plagues on Egypt, Pharaoh still refused to listen to Moses. This cost him greatly – eventually he lost his son to a plague and his army in the Red Sea.

You must remember that you always want to be on God's side, because he always wins. You do this by listening and obeying his commands.

Lord, help me to always listen when you speak to me in your word, when I pray, or when others advise me. I want to be on your side. Amen.

DAVID — GREED

David sent someone to find out about [the woman]. The man said, "Isn't this Bathsheba, the daughter of Eliam and the wife of Uriah the Hittite?" Then David sent messengers to get her. (2 Samuel 11:3-4, NIV)

David was a hero when he was younger, but he got greedy. He was a king, he had lots of money and power, he could have anything he wanted – but he wanted more. He saw Bathsheba and wanted her, but she was married. David had her husband killed and married her. His greed caused him to covet something that wasn't his. He committed both adultery and murder. It wasn't until the prophet came to confront him that he felt guilty and asked for forgiveness. God did forgive him, but David paid for his sin.

It would have been much better for David to be thankful for all that God gave him and not desire something that he shouldn't have. Don't get greedy. When God blesses you, be thankful.

Lord, I don't want to be greedy, so please touch my heart so I will be thankful for what I already have. Amen.

ABSALOM – REBELLION

As they were on the way back to Jerusalem, this report reached David: "Absalom has killed all the king's sons; not one is left alive!" (2 Samuel 13:30, NLT)

King David's son Absalom tried to steal the throne. The Bible describes him as a handsome man who got the people to want him to be king instead of his father. Absalom planned a rebellion to become king; he even killed his own brothers. Eventually, Absalom was caught and killed by another soldier. Rebellion always ends badly.

God does not like it when young people rebel against their parents. You should also not be rebellious at school or against other people who are in authority over you. Rebellion will get you into trouble every time. Be respectful of your parents, your teachers, and the other adults in your life.

Lord, even when my parents upset me, please remind me to be respectful. I don't want to have a rebellious attitude toward those in authority over me. Amen.

THE CRUEL MIDIANITES

That is the story of how the people of Israel defeated Midian, which never recovered. Throughout the rest of Gideon's lifetime – about forty years – there was peace in the land. (Judges 8:28, NLT)

The Midianites were cruel to God's people. They stole from the Israelites and wouldn't allow them to plant fields for food. The Israelites asked God for help, so he raised up a leader named Gideon. Gideon's army defeated the Midianites, and the bad guys never recovered.

God loves his people, and he punishes bad guys who hurt them. You should be excited because now you are one of God's people, so he looks out for you. You should feel loved and safe, because God takes care of those who love him.

Lord, you are so amazing because you look out for me. Thank you so much. Amen.

JEZEBEL – VIOLENCE

Jezebel sent this message to Elijah: "May the gods strike me and even kill me if by this time tomorrow I have not killed you just as you killed them." (1 Kings 19:2, NLT)

Jezebel is one of the wicked people in the Bible. She was very violent and killed lots of people. She even killed several of God's prophets, and she threatened to kill Elijah. But the Bible says that you reap what you sow, which means that you get what you give. Since Jezebel was violent, she died a violent death.

You might know some kids at school who like to start fights. Many times it's the same kids who fight over and over again. If you act violently, others will be violent back to you. Don't be a violent person, because you invite violence to come back at you from others.

Jesus, help me not to be a violent person. Calm my temper and give me wisdom. Amen.

HEROD — FEAR

"Get up," [the angel] said, *"take the child and his mother and escape to Egypt. Stay there until I tell you, for Herod is going to search for the child to kill him."* (Matthew 2:13, NIV)

You would think that everyone would be excited when Jesus was born, right? But not everyone was. In fact, King Herod wanted to kill the baby Jesus because he didn't want anyone threatening his leadership. When the wise men arrived in Jerusalem looking for the "king of the Jews," Herod was afraid that the new king might try to take his throne.

He was so afraid of this little baby that he sent soldiers to kill every baby boy in Bethlehem. Fear can make you do really bad things. You might be afraid that everyone is out to get you or that your friends are always lying. Take a deep breath. Ask God to take away all of your fear. With him on your side, you don't need to be afraid of anything.

God, I don't want to live in fear, so give me your eternal peace. Amen.

JUDAS — BETRAYAL

"What are you willing to give me if I hand him over to you?" So they counted out for him thirty silver coins. From then on Judas watched for an opportunity to hand him over. (Matthew 26:15-16, NIV)

Judas was around Jesus as much as anyone could be. He saw the miracles and he listened to his teachings, but he decided to betray Jesus anyway. All the other disciples ended up doing great things for God and telling many the good news about Jesus, but Judas turned away and betrayed him. He regretted his decision later on, but the damage was already done.

Loyalty is when you stand by someone no matter what happens. For example, if Sean isn't popular at school, then you are being a loyal friend if you stick with him anyway, instead of deciding to only hang out with the cool kids. You would want people to be loyal to you, so do the same for them.

God, I want to be loyal to my friends and family. I know you gave them to me for a reason so I don't want to betray any of them. Amen.

PETER — PEER PRESSURE

After a little while, those standing near said to Peter, "Surely you are one of them, for you are a Galilean." He began to call down curses on himself, and he swore to them, "I don't know this man you're talking about." (Mark 14:70-71, NIV)

Peter was one of Jesus' disciples and became the leader of the early church, but he made a lot of bad decisions. When Jesus was arrested, Peter was seen by some people, but he pretended not to know Jesus. He gave in to peer pressure, which is when you give in to the people around you even if you know it is the wrong thing to do.

Peter didn't want the people around to think he was friends with the man on trial for his life. He was afraid. Peter later asked for forgiveness, but for one night he was not a hero. Don't give in to peer pressure when people try to get you to do things that aren't right. Stick by your beliefs and stand strong for God.

God, I don't want to wimp out and give in to my friends if I know it's the wrong thing to do. Help me to stand my ground when I need to. Amen.

ANANIAS AND SAPPHIRA – LYING

Peter said, "Ananias, why have you let Satan fill your heart? You lied to the Holy Spirit, and you kept some of the money for yourself." (Acts 5:3, NLT)

Ananias and his wife Sapphira gave money to the church, but they lied to the church leaders. They said they gave the church all of the money, but in reality they only gave a portion of the money.

They didn't have to give the church any of the money because it was theirs. But they wanted to look good in front of the rest of the church, so they pretended to give all of the money. Because they lied, they brought judgment on themselves. They both died due to the judgment of the Holy Spirit. Lying is a very big deal and can get you in all sorts of trouble.

Tell the truth, because it's not fun when you get caught lying.

Lord, I want to tell the truth, so help me not to lie. Amen.

SODOM AND GOMORRAH — SIN

The Lord told Abraham, "I have heard a great outcry from Sodom and Gomorrah, because their sin is so flagrant." (Genesis 18:20, NLT)

The two cities of Sodom and Gomorrah were so wicked that God decided to destroy them. The people of those cities sinned in all kinds of terrible ways. Abraham asked God to spare the cities if there were even ten godly people in them. Unfortunately, God couldn't find even ten godly people in the cities. So God destroyed Sodom and Gomorrah because of their sinful ways.

God hates sin. He knows that sin ultimately destroys people. If you're a Christian, you've been forgiven, but you still will battle against sin. Don't allow sin to control your life. God wants you to follow him and live according to his ways. The Holy Spirit will help you stay strong against sin.

Lord, forgive me of my sins and help me to guard myself from letting sin take control of my life. Amen.

BAD THIEF ON THE CROSS — MOCKING

One of the criminals hanging beside him scoffed, "So you're the Messiah, are you? Prove it by saving yourself – and us, too, while you're at it!" (Luke 23:39, NLT)

When Jesus was on the cross, many of the guards and officials mocked him for saying he was a king. Even one of the criminals being crucified beside him also made fun of him. No one realized that the man that they were making fun of could save their lives.

Jesus was made fun of by mean people, so you must remember that God doesn't want you to make fun of people. Since all people are created by God, when you tease and mock others, you are hurting God's creations. Besides, you don't really know who those people are. You don't know the story about their lives. Instead, show kindness. That's what Jesus would want you to do.

Lord, I don't like be teased, and I'm sure you didn't either, so show me how to be a person of kindness. Amen.

PHARISEES – NO FAITH

I warn you – unless your righteousness is better than the righteousness of the teachers of religious law and the Pharisees, you will never enter the Kingdom of Heaven! (Matthew 5:20, NLT)

The Pharisees were some of the religious leaders in Jesus' day. They cared very much about the law. In fact, following laws became more important to them than anything else, and they often accused Jesus of being a lawbreaker. They didn't believe Jesus' teachings because sometimes he taught things that didn't line up with the laws the Pharisees had added to God's law in the Bible.

They were more worried about the appearance of doing good works than about actually doing good works in order to serve God. Jesus taught that you have to believe in your heart that what God says is true and then this should make a difference in how you live. Doing good things isn't enough; your heart and mind must be right.

Jesus, I want to do good things like I'm supposed to, but I also want you to work on my heart and mind to become more like you. Amen.

SAUL (PAUL) — APPROVING SIN

Saul was there, giving approval to [Stephen's] death. On that day a great persecution broke out against the church at Jerusalem, and all except the apostles were scattered throughout Judea and Samaria. (Acts 8:1, NIV)

Paul (who was first called Saul) wrote most of the New Testament and was the main leader who took the gospel to those who weren't Jews. But before Paul was a great apostle, he was an enemy to the church. He didn't kill Stephen for talking about Jesus, but he was with the killers and he gave his approval. Stephen had done nothing wrong except preach the gospel. The Bible says that Saul began arresting Christians and taking them to jail. Eventually, God got hold of him and changed his life.

When you hang around kids who do bad things, you are just as responsible even if you don't do anything. Don't approve of others' sins. Instead, stand up against it.

Lord, help me not to hang around troublemakers. When I see people doing something wrong, help me to speak up for what's right. Amen.

JONADAB – BEING SNEAKY

Amnon had a very crafty friend – his cousin Jonadab. (2 Samuel 13:3, NLT)

You might not have heard of Jonadab, but he was a "crafty" man who probably started a war. He made a sneaky plan to help the king's son Amnon trick his half-sister Tamar. This trick hurt her very badly; in fact, it ruined her life. When Tamar's brother Absalom heard about what Amnon did to his sister, he started a war. Eventually, Absalom killed his half-brother Amnon.

All of this started because Jonadab got other people in trouble. You might know someone like him. When a kid wants to sell you drugs, tells you to skip school, or tries to convince you to do something you know you shouldn't, he is being like Jonadab. You want to stay away from Jonadabs because they end up getting people close to them in a lot of trouble. You don't need sneaky friends.

God, help me to be smart and stay away from anyone who is like Jonadab. I don't want sneaky friends. I want friends who love you. Amen.

NEBUCHADNEZZAR – BEING PUSHY

Nebuchadnezzar said to them, "Is it true, Shadrach, Meshach, and Abednego, that you refuse to worship the gold statue I have set up? I will give you one more chance to bow down and worship the statue ... But if you refuse, you will be thrown immediately into the blazing furnace." (Daniel 3:14-15, NLT)

King Nebuchadnezzar made a big statue and wanted everyone to worship it. Those who refused would be thrown into a blazing furnace. Three young Jewish men refused to bow to the statue because they didn't want to worship an idol. They knew the truth and so refused to do what the king told them to do.

Nebuchadnezzar had the power and authority, but he couldn't force those young men to worship a false god. Being pushy won't get you anywhere. You believe in God and you *know* the truth, but you still can't force others to believe in him. Keep on obeying God and speak up when you get the chance – without being pushy.

God, I want people to know how awesome you are, but help me not to be pushy. Amen.

POTIPHAR'S WIFE – ACCUSER

*When he heard me scream for help,
he left his cloak beside me and ran out
of the house. (Genesis 39:15, NIV)*

Before Joseph became the second most powerful man in Egypt, he led a very difficult life. His brothers sold him into slavery. Then, in Egypt, he was bought by a man named Potiphar and became a servant in his house. Potiphar's wife tried to make Joseph do something bad. Joseph didn't do it, but she accused him of it anyway. So even though Joseph was innocent, he went to jail. The Bible doesn't say what happened to this lying woman, but it does say that Joseph spent two years in jail before he eventually got released. God had a plan for Joseph.

Remember that you shouldn't accuse people of something if it isn't true. That breaks one of God's Ten Commandments – the one that says, "You must not testify falsely against your neighbor" (Exodus 20:16, NLT).

Lord, I know that you love truth and hate lies, so help me to always be honest when I speak. Amen.

SOLDIERS — WANTING MORE STUFF

*After they had nailed him to the cross,
the soldiers gambled for his clothes by
throwing dice. (Matthew 27:35, NLT)*

When Jesus was on the cross, the soldiers took his clothes and gambled to see who would get them. Can you imagine people gambling for the clothes of the Son of God while he was on the cross? Sounds pretty mean, doesn't it? They were more worried about getting stuff (in this case, some used clothes) than the fact that the person who could save their lives was dying before their eyes.

Some people today are just like that. They are more worried about clothes, money, cars, video games, and other stuff than they are about where they will spend eternity. What is more important to you? When you allow possessions to control your life, you forget to serve Jesus. Don't worry so much about how much stuff you can get. Focus on Jesus and he will take care of the rest.

God, I do like getting new things, but I want you to be first. Forgive me for being selfish. Amen.

SIMON – GOD IS NOT FOR SALE

When Simon saw that the Holy Spirit was given when the apostles laid their hands on people, he offered them money to buy this power. (Acts 8:18, NLT)

Simon liked supernatural powers. When he saw the Holy Spirit come down on people when the apostles laid their hands on them, he tried to buy God's powers from the disciples. Simon didn't understand that God is not for sale.

Sometimes people try to make deals with God. For example, a boy who wants a new video game might tell God that if God will give him the new game, then he'll go to church. God is not interested in deals; he wants people to be sold out for him. He doesn't want you to only want his "power," he wants you to want *him* – all of him.

Lord, help me to want all of you. Amen.

JOHN MARK — QUITTING

*Barnabas wanted to take John, also called
Mark, with them, but Paul did not think it
wise to take him, because he had deserted them
in Pamphylia and had not continued with
them in the work.* (Acts 15:37-38, NIV)

John Mark traveled with Paul and Barnabas as
they ministered the gospel to people. But at some
point along the journey, John Mark left Paul and
Barnabas and went back home. Later on, Barnabas wanted to take John Mark on another trip, but
Paul did not. Paul did not think highly of taking
someone who deserted them.

Your reputation is very important. If you quit
things before you finish them, others will think of
you as a quitter. John Mark eventually got another
chance, but it took a while for Paul to trust him
again. Keep your word, and finish the things you
say you will finish.

Jesus, I want to have a good reputation of finishing
my school work, chores, and my job. Please help me.
Amen.

JOAB — FAILING THE SECOND TIME

May their blood be on Joab and his descendants
*forever, and may the L*ORD* grant peace forever*
to David, his descendants, his dynasty,
and his throne. (1 Kings 2:33, NLT)

Joab was a mighty soldier and leader in David's army. When one of David's sons tried to take over as king, Joab didn't join him. Instead, he defended David. But years later, another one of David's sons tried to take David's throne. This time Joab joined the rebellion. Joab had been a loyal warrior for David, but he died a traitor. He didn't stay strong against the devil's temptations.

The devil doesn't just try to get you to sin one time; he will try again and again. Maybe you've been able to stand strong against temptation up until now, but don't let down your guard. The devil will keep trying. So always be aware and watch out for the devil. Be smart and obey God.

Lord, I don't want to be like Joab. I want to be wise every time the enemy tries to tempt me. Amen.

PILATE – DOING NOTHING

"Why?" Pilate demanded. "What crime has he committed?" But the mob roared even louder, "Crucify him!" Pilate sent for a bowl of water and washed his hands before the crowd, saying, "I am innocent of this man's blood. The responsibility is yours!" (Matthew 27:23-24, NLT)

Jesus was brought before Pilate and put on trial, but Pilate didn't think that Jesus had done anything wrong. However, the crowd voted to crucify Jesus. Pilate didn't understand why, but he didn't do anything about it. He had the authority to let Jesus go, but he listened to the crowd. Pilate didn't kill Jesus, but he is just as responsible because he chose not to do anything to stop it.

As you get older, there will be times when you are able to help someone. It will be your choice whether or not you do. Don't be like Pilate, standing aside and refusing to help even if you could. The Bible says that when you help someone, it's like you are helping Jesus himself.

Lord, I want to make a difference. I don't want to be afraid to help those in need. Amen.

JOB'S FRIENDS — ACCUSING GOD

I am angry with you and your two friends, because you have not spoken of me what is right, as my servant Job has. (Job 42:7, NIV)

A lot of bad things happened to Job, and his friends didn't help much at all. They didn't support Job, and they said bad things about him and about God. Job, however, continued to trust in God.

Sometimes when bad things happen, people blame God because they think that he has left them all alone and all the bad things are his fault. If someone blames God for bad things that happen, don't listen to them. When you have tough times, don't blame God. Instead, embrace him as Job did. He is on your side. Always believe the best of God, because he does want the best for you.

Jesus, when bad things happen, I don't want to blame you. Help me to remember how much you love me and want the best for me. Amen.

THE RICH YOUNG MAN – MONEY

When Jesus heard his answer, he said, "There is still one thing you haven't done. Sell all your possessions and give the money to the poor, and you will have treasure in heaven. Then come, follow me." (Luke 18:22, NLT)

A rich man came to Jesus asking how to get to heaven. He said that he had obeyed all of the Ten Commandments. Jesus told him to do one more thing – to sell everything he had and follow him. The rich young man was sad, because he owned a lot of stuff. Jesus cared for him, but he went away upset because he didn't want to sell his stuff and give away the money.

Don't let anything get in your way of following Jesus. The rich man was given an offer to follow Jesus and he refused. He didn't want to give up his stuff. You don't have to give up everything you have, but be careful not to let the stuff you have keep you from following Jesus.

Jesus, please kick out of my life anything that gets in the way of following you. Amen.

ELI — NO SELF-CONTROL

When the messenger mentioned what had happened to the Ark of God, Eli fell backward from his seat beside the gate. He broke his neck and died, for he was old and overweight. He had been Israel's judge for forty years. (1 Samuel 4:18, NLT)

Eli led Israel for forty years, which is a long time, but he might have been able to serve even longer if he had not been so overweight. God loves you no matter what. If you are big or small God loves you the same, but when you are unhealthy, it can limit how much you can do to serve him.

Eli got so overweight that when he fell off a bench, he broke his neck and died. Your body is a temple for the Holy Spirit because Jesus lives inside of you. Do your best to stay healthy by not eating junk food and playing outside more. God gave you your body, and you should take good care of it.

God, help me to be healthy. Help me to eat healthy food and give me chances to play outside more. Amen.

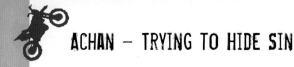

ACHAN – TRYING TO HIDE SIN

Israel violated the instructions about the things set apart for the LORD. A man named Achan had stolen some of these dedicated things, so the LORD was very angry with the Israelites. (Joshua 7:1, NLT)

Achan stole a bunch of stuff – including gold, silver, and a robe – from Jericho when the Israelites defeated the city. God had commanded the soldiers not to take anything because these things were meant for destruction.

Because Achan disobeyed a command, God punished all of Israel. Achan hid the treasures in the ground, thinking no one would find them, but God sees everything. God told Joshua what happened and pointed out Achan. Then Achan and his family were punished with death.

Whenever you do wrong, don't try to hide your sin because God can see it anyway. You can come to God anytime and confess your sins. He is always willing to forgive.

Lord, forgive me of every hidden sin. Help me to remember that I can't hide anything from you. Amen.

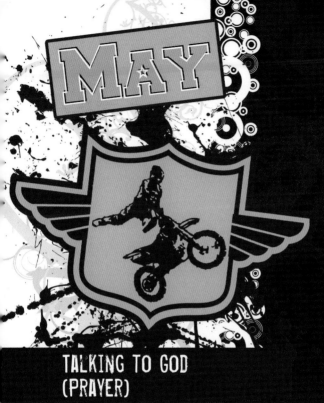

MAY

TALKING TO GOD (PRAYER)

SIMPLE PRAYER

*And when you pray, do not be like the hypocrites,
for they love to pray standing in the synagogues
and on the street corners to be seen by men.
I tell you the truth, they have received their
reward in full. (Matthew 6:5, NIV)*

You shouldn't be scared to pray. It isn't a tough thing to do, because you simply talk to God. In Jesus' day, some religious leaders tried to make it sound tough by praying really long prayers. They also prayed real loud so others could hear them. But Jesus said that he didn't want people to pray that way – to get attention or praise from people.

You don't have to be fancy to talk to God. Don't be afraid that you're not smart enough, that you're too young, or that he won't listen to you. God will hear you. Don't make it difficult. Just talk to God like you would if you were talking to someone who loves you, loves to hear from you, and cares about you – which he does!

Jesus, help me to learn how to pray simply. Remind me that you love to hear from me! Amen.

LONGING PRAYER

*My God, my God, why have you abandoned
me? Why are you so far away when
I groan for help? (Psalm 22:1, NLT)*

God is a big God with big shoulders. That means
he can handle anything you have to say. God
wants to hear from you – he already knows everything anyway, but he still loves it when you talk
to him. When you feel down and sad, tell him
how you feel. Even if you are upset, be honest
about your feelings.

The writer of this psalm, David, was calling out
to God because he felt that God had abandoned
him, that God was far away. You can speak like
this to God. Of course, you should always be
respectful, but don't be afraid to tell God what
you are truly thinking. You might not always feel
like he hears you, but he does. Talk to God every
day. He loves to hear from you.

Lord, I want to give you my biggest fears and trust you
with my tears and anger. Please show me how. Amen.

ANY-TIME PRAYER

My heart has heard you say, "Come and talk with me." And my heart responds, "LORD, I am coming." (Psalm 27:8, NLT)

Dylan was sitting on a hill looking at the big lake and green mountains and he thought about how awesome God is. He told God how he liked all the cool things he made. He thanked God that he could enjoy being able to relax and enjoy the view. Dylan wasn't praying for someone and he wasn't crying out for help. He simply told God what he was thinking at that moment.

You don't have to wait to pray when something is wrong. You can just tell God what you are thinking at any time. He likes it when you talk to him, just like you like to talk to your friends. He wants to be a part of every moment of your life.

Lord, thank you that I can talk to you just like I would talk to my friends. Amen.

PRAYER OF TEARS

David said to God, "I have sinned greatly by doing this. Now, I beg you, take away the guilt of your servant. I have done a very foolish thing." (1 Chronicles 21:8, NIV)

Jackson stole a piece of candy from the local store. At first, all he thought about was how much he loved chocolate, but later on after he had eaten the candy, he felt bad. He felt so bad that he rushed to the store and told the owner what he had done. He cried, because he felt so badly, and he brought some money to pay for the candy.

When you have sinned and you know you have done something wrong, you can ask God for forgiveness. He gave you a conscience to make sure you know when you sin. When you mess up, it is okay to feel bad. Tell God you're sorry, and then say you're sorry to whoever you might have hurt. This will keep you from making the same mistake again.

Lord, I am sorry for doing the things I know I shouldn't have done. Keep me from doing it again. Amen.

PRAYER OF RELINQUISHMENT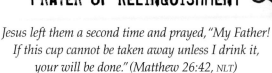

Jesus left them a second time and prayed, "My Father!
If this cup cannot be taken away unless I drink it,
your will be done." (Matthew 26:42, NLT)

Aaron climbed a tree, but slipped and grabbed hold of the tree limb. He was so high up that his dad had to climb halfway to be able to reach him. His dad told him to grab his hand, but Aaron was afraid, because that meant he'd have to let go of the tree branch.

Sometimes you might feel like this in your life. When you need help from God, you have to reach out to him, but that means that you must let go of anything that would stop you from totally trusting God. Aaron trusted his dad and they both made it down safely. If you trust God, you too will be safe.

Is there anything you need to let go of in order to be able to trust God better?

God, help me to let go of anything that keeps me from grabbing hold of you. Amen.

TRANSFORMING PRAYER

For when I tried to keep the law, it condemned me.
So I died to the law – I stopped trying to meet all
its requirements – so that I might live for God.
(Galatians 2:19, NLT)

Transforming prayers ask God to help you become more like Jesus. Becoming like Jesus is becoming the very best you can be – the person God created you to be. Take the example of a caterpillar. Caterpillars look like fuzzy worms with legs, but they end up becoming butterflies. They stop crawling, they grow wings, and they fly!

But what if a caterpillar decided he didn't want to change at all? He'd miss out on flying; he'd be stuck on the ground. As a Christian you are supposed to become more and more like Jesus, but if you stop growing then you will miss out on being all that God wants you to be. So keep on praying for God to transform you to be more like Jesus so that you, too, can live for God.

God, transform my heart, mind, and spirit to be more and more like Jesus every day. Amen.

COVENANT PRAYER

He says, "I will declare your name to my brothers; in the presence of the congregation I will sing your praises." (Hebrews 2:12, NIV)

Kenny and Cole promised each other that they would be best friends always – even as they got old and had their own families. They kept their promise, because they are still best friends even though they have gotten older, married, and had kids and grandkids of their own.

As you grow up, remember that promises are important. The biggest promise you can make is called a covenant. When you ask Jesus to be your Savior, you make a covenant to him. This means that you pledge your allegiance to him as your King, Savior, and best friend. When you make a promise to God, he expects you to keep it, just like Kenny and Cole kept theirs.

And just as they are glad to tell others about their friendship, you can tell others about your friendship with Jesus.

Jesus, I pledge my life to you. I want to be with you always. Amen.

PRAYER OF WORSHIP

The LORD is my strength and my shield;
my heart trusts in him, and I am helped.
My heart leaps for joy and I will give
thanks to him in song. (Psalm 28:7, NIV)

In the Bible, David is mentioned several times as a big-time worshipper. In the book of Psalms, you can read a lot of David's prayers to God. When you worship God through prayer, you are simply telling him how awesome he is and how much you love him. The Bible says many times that God loves those who worship him.

You should go to church and worship God there, but that doesn't have to be the only time you worship. You don't need a certain place or a certain time to worship God. You can just go by yourself to your room, kneel beside your bed, and tell him how grateful you are for him. That is worship. When you do this, like David, your heart will leap for joy.

God, you are wonderful. I don't have enough words to say how much you mean to me, but I love you and am thankful for you. Amen.

PRAYER OF REST

Take my yoke upon you. Let me teach you, because I am humble and gentle at heart, and you will find rest for your souls. (Matthew 11:29, NLT)

Martin had a lot on his mind – he had a test to study for, a game to plan for, and a million chores to do around the house. Instead of stressing out, he took a few minutes, laid on his bed, and focused on Jesus. He prayed and spoke out loud what Jesus was like, "Jesus was calm, peaceful, and loving … " He asked God to help him "find rest for his soul." As he began to focus on Jesus, he began to calm down. Suddenly all the things he had to get done didn't seem so bad anymore.

He started his tasks. With his focus on Jesus, he was able to stay calm and get it all done. When you feel like you have too much to do and too many things on your mind, take a few minutes and focus on Jesus. Ask him to give rest to your soul. You will relax and be able to get started on your tasks knowing that Jesus is with you.

Jesus, you are easy-going and always handle things well. Help me to be able to be calm like you. Amen.

SACRAMENTAL PRAYER

As they were eating, Jesus took some bread and blessed it. Then he broke it in pieces and gave it to the disciples, saying, "Take this and eat it, for this is my body." (Matthew 26:26, NLT)

During that last supper, Jesus shared bread and wine with his disciples. He compared the bread to his body and the wine to his blood. Jesus used symbols like this to help teach those who followed him. Churches today still have Communion to help teach and remind us what Jesus did for us.

When you pray the words Jesus spoke, you are giving honor to the amazing things Jesus did for you. These words help you connect with him on a deeper level. You might not understand all of this yet, but just remember that Communion is a very special celebration. When you celebrate Communion, you are remembering Jesus and what he did for you.

Jesus, help me to realize the importance of the bread, the wine, and the words you spoke during the last supper. Amen.

CONTINUAL PRAYER

Pray continually. (1 Thessalonians 5:17, NIV)

The Bible says that you should pray continually. That means that you should not stop praying. How can you do that? Obviously you have to do other things like go to school and do your homework and your chores. But you can "pray continually" by keeping an attitude of prayer all day long. When you have this attitude, you might be surprised at how it changes things in your everyday life.

If you are in class, say a quick prayer for your teacher. If you are playing video games online, pray for those you are playing against. Prayers don't have to be long and they don't even have to be really loud. Just pray simple prayers throughout your day and focus on Jesus every chance you get.

God, I want to be someone who is known as a "pray-er." I don't want to stop praying no matter what I am busy with. Amen.

PRAYER OF THE HEART

O Lord, hear my plea for justice. Listen to my cry for help. Pay attention to my prayer, for it comes from honest lips. (Psalm 17:1, NLT)

Hunter went on a long journey where he saw many great things and met some interesting people, but he also faced hard times. There were times when Hunter missed his family greatly and felt that he was alone. Sometimes he needed help, but there was no one to call on for help.

Eventually Hunter returned home and told his dad everything that had happened. He wished that he could have talked to his dad during the tough times, the lonely times, the times when he needed help.

You don't need to wait to talk to God. You can talk to him anytime, all the time. You can have a heart-to-heart with God whenever you want, and you can share everything with him. Don't wait! Talk to him now.

God, I am so excited about _____ in my life, and I am looking forward to _____. Please be with me and thank you for listening. Amen.

BIBLE PRAYER

Sustain me, and I will be rescued; then I will meditate continually on your decrees. (Psalm 119:117, NLT)

Ethan was always scared of riding the school bus. Some of the kids were mean and he didn't want to get teased. His Sunday school teacher gave him a verse and told him to pray it and think of it any time he was scared. Ethan kept this verse on his mind the whole bus trip. He whispered it over and over to himself.

Not only did he feel better, but he wasn't afraid to stick up for the other kids when they were getting teased. Just like the psalmist wrote, Ethan meditated on (meaning he thought about and kept his mind on) verses from God's word and he was helped.

When you think and pray the words from the Bible, you allow God's promises to come alive in your life.

Lord, I want to focus on your word so that your promises become true in my life. Amen.

SILENT PRAYER

As soon as Jesus heard the news [of John the Baptist's death], he left in a boat to a remote area to be alone. (Matthew 14:13, NLT)

Fredrick and his dad were fishing. Fred liked to spend time with his dad. They didn't even have to talk, because just hanging out and enjoying the view was enough to make lasting memories. You can hang out with God just like Fred did with his dad. You don't have to talk either. You can go to your room or sit under a tree and just be silent.

To start doing this, ask God to be with you as you spend quiet time with him. Then think about the wonders of God and what he means to you. Silent prayer shows God that you put all of the other things in your life on hold to focus only on him. Turn off the TV, computer, and phone and just silently pray to God.

God, I ask you to be with me as I focus in on you and only you. Amen.

EVERYTHING PRAYER

Until now you have not asked for anything in my name. Ask and you will receive, and your joy will be complete. (John 16:24, NIV)

Edward prayed about everything. When he had a good game, he thanked God for being able to do well. Before he ate his food, he would pray to bless the food and thank God for providing it. Edward would pray for people he saw at the store even if he didn't know them.

He even prayed when he saw how ants work – he prayed that he would also be a hard worker like the ants he saw. He prayed about simple things all the time. You don't have to wait for something big to happen before you pray. You can pray for the simplest things that happen in your day.

Jesus, thank you for _____ (something small), and bless _____ (someone you see every day), and help me to be more like _____ (someone that teaches you to be more like God). Amen.

PRAYER OF REQUEST

[Hannah] made this vow: "O LORD of Heaven's Armies, if you will look upon my sorrow and answer my prayer and give me a son, then I will give him back to you. He will be yours for his entire lifetime." (1 Samuel 1:11, NLT)

C.J. always looked up to his older brother, and he loved celebrating Christmas with his family. This year, C.J. was afraid that his brother would miss Christmas because he was in the army serving his country. C.J. prayed and prayed that his big brother would make it home for Christmas.

On Christmas day, a miracle happened. His big brother made it home for the family celebration! This type of praying is a prayer of request. It is when you ask God for something for yourself. C.J. wanted to see his brother again, and God allowed it to happen. What do you want? Don't be afraid to ask God for something that is really important to you. He might say yes, he might say no, but you won't know unless you ask.

God, the thing I want the most is _____.
Please, if it is in your will, allow it to happen. Amen.

PRAYING FOR OTHERS

Pray this way for kings and all who are in authority so that we can live peaceful and quiet lives marked by godliness and dignity. (1 Timothy 2:2, NLT)

After Christmas, C.J.'s big brother went back to his post and continued to serve his country. C.J. was worried about his brother, so he prayed every morning when he woke up and every night when he went to sleep that God would protect his brother from danger.

Praying for others is sometimes the only thing you can do. If something is out of your control and the only thing you can do is trust God, then pray as much as you can for others. Praying for others shows that you care about them. Some only pray for themselves, but God likes it when you are not selfish and you pray for the needs of other people as well.

God, right now I really pray your blessing over _____ _____ (someone you know who has a special need). Amen.

HEALING PRAYER

By faith in the name of Jesus, this man whom
you see and know was made strong. It is
Jesus' name and the faith that comes through
him that has given this complete healing to
him, as you can all see. (Acts 3:16, NIV)

Jesus was well known for healing people from sickness. After he went back to heaven, his disciples also prayed for healing over those who needed it. Many people were healed when the disciples prayed for them, but only because of the name of Jesus.

Because Jesus died for sins and rose again from the dead, Jesus has the power over life and death. When believers pray for healing, they pray over the sick and ask for healing in the name of Jesus. When you pray, don't forget that the power in your prayers comes from the name of Jesus.

Jesus, I praise your name above all names, and I thank you for the power of it, too. Amen.

THE PRAYER OF SUFFERING

In my distress I called to the LORD; I cried to my God for help. From his temple he heard my voice; my cry came before him, into his ears. (Psalm 18:6, NIV)

Todd and his buddies were riding their bikes on trails in the mountains, but they all wrecked their bikes and were hurt. They were in so much pain that they couldn't walk. Todd prayed that God would heal his friends and him from the pain so they could get back home. Todd hurt so much that he cried while he prayed. He kept praying over and over again.

A prayer of suffering is when you give your pain or someone else's pain over to God. Pain is a part of life. At some point you will be hurt and you must trust God to take care of you. It might be physical pain or it might be emotional pain, but either way don't forget to pray and give it over to God.

Lord, right now I want to give you my pain. I want to give you any kind of pain I have right now. Amen.

PRAYER OF AUTHORITY

Now Elijah, who was from Tishbe in Gilead, told King Ahab, "As surely as the LORD, the God of Israel, lives – the God I serve – there will be no dew or rain during the next few years until I give the word!" (1 Kings 17:1, NLT)

In the Old Testament, praying the authority of God over a situation happened a lot. Because King Ahab had been so evil, Elijah prayed that no rain would come. He wanted to prove to Ahab that God is in control and that Ahab should worship only God.

Elijah used the name of God to command something to be done, and it happened! This was a prayer of authority. God listened to Elijah; it didn't rain for a long time. God has all the authority in every situation. Nothing is too tough for him.

God, I ask that you would take control of my current situation. I pray your will, in Jesus name. Amen.

RADICAL PRAYER

Reach down from heaven and rescue me;
rescue me from deep waters, from the power
of my enemies. (Psalm 144:7, NLT)

Joe saw on TV that a big earthquake had left a lot of people without homes and without food. Right then, Joe prayed a radical prayer for all those hurt people and asked God to help them.

Radical prayers ask God to change big things. Praying that God would feed the hungry and end starvation is one example of radical prayer. Even if you are thousands of miles away, you can make a difference in the lives of other people by praying a radical prayer for them.

Remember, God loves it when people pray and trust him – and he loves radical prayers.

God, I ask that you would minister to those in _____
_____ (pick a country or city). I ask that you help them. Amen.

THE LORD'S PRAYER

This, then, is how you should pray: "Our Father in heaven, hallowed be your name." (Matthew 6:9, NIV)

Becket didn't know how to get home from his new school, so a kid named William drew him a map to show him how to get home. Eventually, he learned the right way on his own. If you don't know how to pray, don't worry. Jesus gave you a map to follow to help you pray.

The Lord's Prayer in Matthew 6 shows you the most important parts of praying. It starts with focusing on God and talking about how holy he is ("hallowed" is another word for "holy"). So when you pray, start out as Jesus did in the Lord's Prayer by focusing on God and how awesome he is. Then you can pray about God's kingdom coming, ask him for the things you need, and pray for forgiveness. Follow the map Jesus gave you!

God, thank you for this prayer map. You think of everything! Amen.

WHAT IS PRAYER?

If only I knew where to find God,
I would go to his court. (Job 23:3, NLT)

When Conor got home from school, he talked on the phone with his dad for a little while. After that, he chatted online with his buddy Joshua. Later, he played an online game with Chad. Conor spent his afternoon talking with three people in three different ways.

Prayer is like that with God. There are different ways to talk to him and, since God is everywhere, you can talk to him from anywhere. You don't need a phone, computer, video game, or even electricity. You don't need to stand or kneel. You don't have to be in a church. All you need is the willingness to talk to him. Prayer isn't complicated. It is just talking to God.

God, I want to pray a lot, so remind me that I can pray anywhere and anytime. Thanks! Amen.

HOW SHOULD YOU PRAY?

May you hear the humble and earnest requests from me and your people Israel when we pray toward this place. Yes, hear us from heaven where you live, and when you hear, forgive. (2 Chronicles 6:21, NLT)

Bryden met the president of his country. He was very nervous. When the president spoke to him, Bryden would answer, "Yes sir" and "No sir." He was respectful because the Bible says to honor your leaders, and he was also humble.

When you pray, remember that you are coming to the King of the universe. Your attitude matters. You should come respectfully and humbly. The most important thing isn't whether or not you pray the right way, it's whether or not you pray with the right heart. If you go to God with a humble heart and show a high level of respect, he will hear your prayers.

God, when I come to you, remind me to come with the right attitude – respectful and humble. Amen.

PRAYING WITH OTHERS

Though one may be overpowered, two can defend themselves. A cord of three strands is not quickly broken. (Ecclesiastes 4:12, NIV)

Patrick was playing tug-of-war with two kids from his class. They were beating him because there were two of them, but only one of him. Then two of Patrick's friends came by and started to help him pull the rope. They won because three people have more strength than one person or even two people.

Prayer is the same way. You don't always have to pray by yourself. When you pray with others, God says he is in your presence. Jesus said, "Where two or three gather together as my followers, I am there among them" (Matthew 18:20, NLT). Do you have some friends you can pray with? God will be right there among your group as you pray. Isn't that amazing?

God, show me some good friends to pray with. When we do pray, please hear us and work on our behalf. Amen.

THE POWER OF PRAYER

Confess your sins to each other and pray for each other so that you may be healed. The earnest prayer of a righteous person has great power and produces wonderful results. (James 5:16, NLT)

All throughout the Bible God describes and shows the power of prayer. Many people in the Bible saw amazing answers to their prayers. But not only do the famous people from the Bible get their prayers heard, you do, too.

You don't have to be famous to be heard by God. You don't have to be a superhero. In fact, the quiet prayers you pray softly in your room before you go to bed have great power. Every prayer grabs the attention of God.

Lord, help me to become a mighty man of prayer. Amen.

COMFORT OF PRAYER

I pray that God, the source of hope, will fill you completely with joy and peace because you trust in him. Then you will overflow with confident hope through the power of the Holy Spirit. (Romans 15:13, NLT)

Joe was scared of the dark. He knew he was old enough not to be afraid, but he couldn't help it. When he heard noises, he would worry. When his dad came to talk to him and prayed over him, Joe felt so much better. All of a sudden, the dark didn't seem so bad.

Praying to God also brings comfort all by itself. Prayer often makes you feel better just for doing it. When you pray, you have a direct connection with God. When you are connected to the Maker of the universe, you shouldn't be surprised if praying to him makes you feel better!

Lord, thank you for the comfort I feel when I pray to you. Thank you for giving me a direct connection to you. Amen.

HOW DOES GOD RESPOND?

Then the LORD said to Moses, "Has my arm lost its power? Now you will see whether or not my word comes true!" (Numbers 11:23, NLT)

When you pray, God responds in a few different ways. Sometimes he intervenes in the situation you are praying about. Other times the Holy Spirit speaks to your heart and gives you an answer. But the main way that God reveals himself is through his word. By reading the Bible, you will discover most of the answers you are looking for.

When you feel alone, the Bible tells you that he sticks closer than a brother. If you don't feel loved, the Bible says God loved you so much that he gave his only Son for you. If you worry about your future, the Bible says that God will guide you and show you the way that you should go. The important thing to remember is that God will always hear and he will always answer.

Lord, help me to pray to you and listen for your answers. Remind me that you are closer to me than a brother. Amen.

THE BEST WAY TO LEARN TO PRAY

I keep praying to you, LORD, hoping this time you will show me favor. In your unfailing love, O God, answer my prayer with your sure salvation. (Psalm 69:13, NLT)

Kevin was trying to learn how to skateboard, but he kept falling on his face. Some of the kids laughed at him, but not Luke. Luke was the best skater around. He told Kevin that learning wasn't easy, but that he just had to keep on trying. So Kevin kept skating and, little by little, he got better and better.

Prayer is the same way. You learn to pray by praying. When you first start, you might feel a bit weird, but don't let that stop you. If you keep on praying, you will build up your confidence. God loves to hear you pray, even if you don't have all the perfect words. Just talk to him. That's what matters most.

God, give me the words to pray the way you want me to pray. Amen.

PRAY AT ALL TIMES

Don't worry about anything; instead, pray about everything. Tell God what you need, and thank him for all he has done. (Philippians 4:6, NLT)

Brad was at church, but he wasn't listening or praying like he should because he was mad at his friend Tom. Tom told the pastor that Brad broke the church window. It was an accident, of course, but Brad was upset at Tom. So he sat in church and couldn't pray because he was mad.

Sometimes you might not feel like praying. You might be angry, sad, or hopeless, but the times you don't feel like praying are often the times when you need to pray the most. When you don't feel like praying the next time, just take a moment and pray a quick prayer for God to help you feel like praying! God knows everything anyway, but he still wants to hear from you.

Lord, I don't feel like praying right now, but help me because I need it. Amen.

WHEN GOD SAYS NO

When you ask, you do not receive, because you ask with wrong motives. (James 4:3, NIV)

There were three boys who wanted their teacher to give them an apple, but the teacher had only one apple. The first boy asked for the apple, then the second boy asked for it, but the third boy didn't ask anything. The teacher gave the apple to the second boy. Why? Well, the teacher knew the boys. She knew the first boy only wanted the apple so he could throw it at people. The third boy never even asked, so of course she didn't give it to him. When God says no to a prayer that you have prayed, it may be because he knows that the answer would only end up hurting you or those around you. Or maybe he knows that your motives aren't right.

Sometimes you don't get what you want because you never even asked. God is a good God, but he also knows what's best for you.

Lord, I want a lot of things, but I trust that you will answer my prayers best, even if your answer is no. Amen.

JUNE

SOVEREIGN COMPANY

HEROES OF GOD
(BIG PLAYERS IN THE
BIBLE AND THEIR LIVES)

ABRAHAM

Finally, Abraham said, "Lord, please don't be angry with me if I speak one more time. Suppose only ten are found there?" And the LORD replied, "Then I will not destroy it for the sake of the ten." (Genesis 18:32, NLT)

God used Abraham to be the ancestor of all the Israelites, and he had a son in his old age. God chose Abraham because he had great faith. Abraham prayed hard for people. The cities of Sodom and Gomorrah were wicked and sinful places. God planned to punish them, but Abraham had compassion on the people and asked God to spare them if he could find ten good people there.

God listened to Abraham and promised that even if there were ten righteous people in the cities, he wouldn't destroy them. Unfortunately, the cities were so evil that God still destroyed them. Abraham was a great hero because of his faith and his willingness to intercede for others. You, too, can pray for others.

Lord, give me a heart to pray for other people to turn their hearts to you. Amen.

MOSES

God said to Moses, "I AM WHO I AM. This is what you are to say to the Israelites: 'I AM has sent me to you.'" (Exodus 3:14, NIV)

Before Moses led the Israelites out of slavery, he was a shepherd for forty years. One day Moses saw a burning bush, but the fire did not hurt the bush. Then Moses heard God calling to him. God wanted Moses to deliver the Israelites out of slavery in Egypt. That was a very big task and Moses at first didn't feel like he was worthy. But Moses listened to God and obeyed, and became a great hero.

Like Moses, you can listen to God's voice because God speaks to you, too. He probably won't use a burning bush; most likely, he will speak to you through the Bible, his word. Moses did not have a Bible to rely on, but you do. God will speak to you when you read his word. Your job? Well, that's like Moses' job too – you need to obey.

God, like Moses I want to hear your words and I want to obey. Please use me to tell others about your love and your desire to free them from sin. Amen.

NOAH

God said to Noah, "I have decided to destroy all living creatures. Build a large boat from cypress wood and waterproof it with tar, inside and out." (Genesis 6:13-14, NLT)

Noah is famous because he saved his family and the animals on the earth by building an ark to protect them from the flood. That's a very cool story, but have you ever thought about how long it took Noah to build the ark? The ark is a very big boat. It had to be so big that he could fit two of every type of animal on earth. God gave Noah the specifics and then he began to build.

The Bible doesn't say how long it took Noah to build the ark, but it took at least several years. During that time, Noah faced teasing from his neighbors who thought he was crazy. But Noah kept building because he trusted God. Some things that God has asked you to do might take a long time. But stay faithful to God and keep doing the things he calls you to do.

God, help me to work hard. I want you to use me. Amen.

JOSEPH

Joseph replied, "Don't be afraid of me. Am I God, that I can punish you? You intended to harm me, but God intended it all for good. He brought me to this position so I could save the lives of many people." (Genesis 50:19-20, NLT)

When Joseph was young, his brothers were jealous of him. One day they got so mad at him that they sold him to be a slave to some passing traders. Then they lied to their father, telling him that Joseph had been killed by a wild animal.

God looked out for Joseph after his brothers sold him. He was noticed as a hard worker and eventually became the second most powerful man in Egypt. But the reason Joseph is a hero is because – even though he became powerful – he forgave his brothers. He understood that even though his brothers had meant to hurt him, God meant it for good. When people hurt you, remember Joseph's example. Forgiving someone might be hard, but it is the right thing to do.

Heavenly Father, help me not to hold grudges against people. Help me to shine your love. Amen.

SAMSON

[The angel] said to [Samson's mother], "You will conceive and give birth to a son. Now then, drink no wine or other fermented drink and do not eat anything unclean, because the boy will be a Nazirite of God from birth until the day of his death." (Judges 13:7, NIV)

You probably remember Samson as the strongest man in the Bible. He took out a bunch of soldiers just with the jawbone of a donkey.

From even before Samson was born, God said that Samson should not eat some types of foods, he should never cut his hair, and he shouldn't drink wine. Then God would make him a special warrior who would save his people from their enemies. Samson is a hero because, even though he sometimes did things wrong, in the end he used his strength for God.

You may not be strong like Samson, but God has given you special gifts. God wants you to be different. He gave you your gifts to use for him.

Jesus, I want to please you. Show me my special gifts and how to use them to honor you. Amen.

DAVID

[David said], "The LORD who delivered me from the paw of the lion and the paw of the bear will deliver me from the hand of this Philistine." Saul said to David, "Go, and the LORD be with you." (1 Samuel 17:37, NIV)

David was confident that he could beat Goliath, but all of the other soldiers were afraid to fight one-on-one with this enemy soldier who also happened to be a nine-foot-tall giant.

When he had been a shepherd watching over his sheep, David had beaten a bear and a lion, so he knew God was on his side and would protect him. David is a hero because of his complete faith in God and his refusal to be afraid. He knew that the enemy soldier was making fun of God's people and that God would beat the giant. So, unafraid for his own life, David took his slingshot and five stones and went out to the field.

The devil wants to make you afraid of everything. But remember that with God, you don't need to be afraid. No giant is too big for God!

Help me, Lord, not to live in fear. I want to be brave and trust you like David did. Amen.

DANIEL

Daniel was determined not to defile himself by eating the food and wine given to them by the king. He asked the chief of staff for permission not to eat these unacceptable foods. (Daniel 1:8, NLT)

In the Old Testament, God commanded his people to only eat certain foods. When Daniel was taken prisoner and sent to another country, the king there provided food for his new servants that included some of the forbidden foods. Daniel stuck by God's command and asked that he could eat only foods that were allowed. This might not seem like a risk to you, but back then, kings might kill prisoners for asking for special treatment.

Daniel could have just decided that food wasn't that big a deal – certainly not worth dying over. But Daniel wanted to obey God. He is a hero because he stood up for his beliefs even if it meant dying for them. Being a Christian means that you must stand up for your beliefs. God is honored when you do.

Jesus, give me the strength to stand up for you. Amen.

SHADRACH, MESHACH, AND ABEDNEGO

Shadrach, Meshach and Abednego replied to the king, "O Nebuchadnezzar, we do not need to defend ourselves before you in this matter." (Daniel 3:16, NIV)

Shadrach, Meshach, and Abednego were young Hebrew men who had been captured by another country and put to work in the king's palace. The king of this new country wanted them to worship an idol of himself, but the three young men refused because they only worshipped God.

The king got so mad that he commanded that they be thrown into a furnace. You probably know the story – they lived because God protected them. But you might not know the other part of the story. The three young men told the king that they did not need to defend themselves before him because they knew that God would defend them. When you are made fun of or are accused of something you didn't do, don't worry about defending yourself. Let God take care of you.

Heavenly Father, if others tell rumors about me or accuse me of something, help me not to argue or get upset. I want others to see you working in me. Amen.

PETER

"Yes, come," Jesus said. So Peter went over the side of the boat and walked on the water toward Jesus. (Matthew 14:29, NLT)

When his disciples were sailing in a storm, Jesus came to them, walking on the water. Peter saw Jesus and asked if he, too, could walk on the water. Jesus told him to come. Peter climbed over the side of the boat and started to walk on water. But when he saw the waves, he got scared and started to sink. Jesus grabbed him, and they both climbed into the boat.

Peter seems to have been brave at first (after all, he was the only disciple who dared to get out of the boat), but he got scared when he saw the waves coming up around him. Some people are scared all of the time and never trust God. Others start to trust God but get scared when they see trouble. God wants you to trust him at all times.

Jesus, I want to trust you enough to do what you call me to do, but sometimes I am afraid. Please help me to be brave and have lots of faith in you! Amen.

PAUL

Upon receiving such orders, [the jailer] put them in the inner cell and fastened their feet in the stocks. About midnight Paul and Silas were praying and singing hymns to God, and the other prisoners were listening to them. (Acts 16:24-25, NIV)

Paul was arrested for telling others about Jesus, but that never stopped him. The jailer knew Paul had not done anything against the law, but he was commanded to guard Paul and Silas carefully. Paul did not get depressed or angry at God. Paul is a hero because he always used every situation to tell others about Jesus.

He and Silas sang hymns and praised God even though they were in chains. When bad things happen, don't get angry and upset. Instead, find a way to thank God and tell others about all that he has done for you. What you are going through right now may not be what you wanted, but God may have a way for you to share about him!

God, I know I can't control anything, so please use me. Help me to know what to say and what to do even when I don't understand. Amen.

STEPHEN

*As they stoned him, Stephen prayed, "Lord Jesus,
receive my spirit." He fell to his knees, shouting,
"Lord, don't charge them with this sin!"
And with that, he died. (Acts 7:59-60, NLT)*

Stephen told others about Jesus. He wasn't an apostle; in fact, he was chosen to help serve the people in the church. He told the good news about Jesus to anyone who would listen. Some people didn't like what Stephen was saying, so they paid a few guys to lie and accuse Stephen of breaking the law. Because of the lies, Stephen was killed.

But just before he died, Stephen did an amazing thing – he prayed for the people who were killing him! Some things in life are out of your control. If the kids in your neighborhood tease you, don't get angry with them. Instead, like Stephen, say a prayer for them. If a relative makes fun of you because of your belief in Jesus, don't get angry. Instead, say a prayer that your relative will one day come to know Jesus just as you have.

Jesus, help me to pray for others to know you. Amen.

GIDEON

"But Lord," Gideon replied, "how can I rescue Israel? My clan is the weakest in the whole tribe of Manasseh, and I am the least in my entire family!" (Judges 6:15, NLT)

God can use anybody. He is just looking for people who love him and are willing to trust him. He can use you if you let him. Gideon was the smallest kid of his family and his family was the weakest of all the other families in their tribe, so when God told him he was going to use him, Gideon was a little scared. He thought maybe God was making a mistake. But God wasn't.

He chose Gideon and used him to conquer the enemies of Israel. God used Gideon, and he can use you too. It doesn't matter if you are really young, or short, or small, or poor. If you love him and are willing to trust him, God can use you to do great things. Do you love God? Do you want to obey him? If so, you are off to a great start already!

God, please use me. I want to obey you, so let me know what you want me to do. Amen.

JOSEPH

After he had considered this, an angel of the Lord appeared to him in a dream and said, "Joseph son of David, do not be afraid to take Mary home as your wife, because what is conceived in her is from the Holy Spirit." (Matthew 1:20, NIV)

Mary and Joseph planned to be married, but Joseph got a little nervous when he learned that Mary was pregnant. An angel told him that everything was okay and that Joseph should still marry the young woman he was engaged to. Joseph did as God said: He married Mary and acted as Jesus' stepfather. Joseph doesn't get talked about a lot in the Bible, but he was important to Jesus' life.

God chose Mary to be Jesus' mother, but he also chose Joseph to be his earthly dad. Joseph had to swallow his pride to marry this young woman who was already pregnant. And he did it because God told him to. Joseph is a hero because he listened to God – even when what God said to do was going to be difficult.

God, help me to always listen to what you want me to do. Give me the faith to obey. Amen.

THE ROMAN OFFICER

When Jesus heard this, he was astonished and said to those following him, "I tell you the truth, I have not found anyone in Israel with such great faith." (Matthew 8:10, NIV)

A Roman army officer asked Jesus to heal his servant who was very sick. Jesus said he would go and heal the servant, but the officer knew that Jesus did not have to visit the sick servant to be able to heal him.

He knew that Jesus could heal him with just a word right from where he was standing. Jesus was amazed at the faith of this man. In fact, he said this Roman officer showed more faith than the Jewish people who should have recognized Jesus as their Messiah.

The soldier's name is not mentioned, but he is one of the few people who Jesus talks about as having great faith. If you want Jesus to marvel at your faith, then trust the words he left for you and believe them.

God, I want to be like the soldier and believe in your great power. Amen.

ZACCHAEUS

Zacchaeus stood up and said to the Lord, "Look, Lord! Here and now I give half of my possessions to the poor, and if I have cheated anybody out of anything, I will pay back four times the amount." (Luke 19:8, NIV)

Zacchaeus was a tax collector – not exactly a popular man in his city because tax collectors often cheated people out of money. But when Jesus arrived in Jericho, he called up to Zacchaeus (who was up in a tree to see over the crowd). Jesus wanted to spend time with Zacchaeus. And Jesus changed the tax collector's life.

In fact, Zacchaeus announced that he was also going to give half of his wealth to the poor and he was going to repay anyone he had cheated. Not only was he going to repay, but he was also going to repay four times the amount! Zacchaeus is a hero because he saw what he was doing wrong and he let Jesus change his life. Then he worked hard to make things right. When Jesus points out to you something that you're doing wrong, be like Zacchaeus and make things right.

Jesus, help me to make wrong things right. Amen.

JONAH

"Throw me into the sea," Jonah said, "and it will become calm again. I know that this terrible storm is all my fault." (Jonah 1:12, NLT)

God told Jonah to go to Nineveh and preach, but Jonah got on a ship to sail the other way because he wanted to hide from God. But God sent a storm, and everyone on the ship was afraid. Jonah admitted that the storm was his fault and told the sailors to throw him overboard. When Jonah went into the water, the storm stopped. You probably know the rest of the story – that Jonah got swallowed by a big fish. Eventually, he did go to Nineveh and God used him to help the people of that city repent.

Jonah made a mistake when he tried to run from God, but he admitted that he was to blame for the storm. You should always obey God, but if you do make a mistake, turn back to God right away. You wouldn't want others to get hurt by something that was your fault.

God, help me to have the courage to admit when I make mistakes. Amen.

ELIJAH

*Then [Elijah] cried out to the L*ORD*, "O L*ORD *my God, have you brought tragedy also upon this widow I am staying with, by causing her son to die?" Then he stretched himself out on the boy three times and cried to the L*ORD*, "O L*ORD *my God, let this boy's life return to him!" (1 Kings 17:20-21, NIV)*

A woman's son died, and she was very sad about it. Elijah was a good friend to her, and he also was very sad when the son died. So he prayed and prayed to God – in fact, he cried out to the Lord because of the tragedy. God listened to Elijah and brought the young boy back to life.

In your life, you will meet people who are very sad because terrible tragedies have happened to them. Like Elijah, pray for those hurting people. Pray that God would touch them, comfort them, and help them. Many kids pray only for themselves, but be different. Pray for the needs of other people. God answers those who seek him.

Lord, I don't want to be selfish in my prayers. Help me to be sensitive to other people's needs so I can pray for them, too. Amen.

★ ★ ★

ELISHA

Elisha sent a messenger out to him with this message: "Go and wash yourself seven times in the Jordan River. Then your skin will be restored, and you will be healed of your leprosy." (2 Kings 5:10, NLT)

Naaman was an important man who wanted to be healed of his disease. He went to Elisha for healing, but Elisha did not treat Naaman any differently than he would anybody else. Naaman expected to get treated better because he was an important person. He didn't like it that Elisha just sent a messenger to tell him to go wash in the river. But Naaman did, and he was healed. God healed him because he obeyed Elisha's orders, not because he was better than anyone else.

You probably know lots of different people – some are more popular, some have more money, some are better looking. God doesn't want you to pick favorites. In fact, God wants you to treat everyone equally. Be kind to everyone.

God, help me to treat everyone fairly. I don't want to pick favorites, so please show me how you see all people in the same way – as people you love. Amen.

JOSHUA

*Moses did as the LORD commanded. He presented
Joshua to Eleazar the priest and the whole community.
Moses laid his hands on him and commissioned him
to lead the people, just as the LORD had commanded
through Moses. (Numbers 27:22-23, NLT)*

Moses had led the Israelites for a very long time.
He took on Pharaoh and led the Israelites out
of Egypt. Eventually, though, Moses got old
and needed someone to succeed him. God chose
Joshua to lead his people into the promised land.
Who was Joshua? He was Moses' assistant. He
served Moses and helped him.

If you want to lead people, you must first be
willing to serve. When you show yourself trustworthy or loyal, then God can use you for other
things. Work hard at every job you have and be
willing to serve other people. Then, like Joshua,
you will be in a good position to take on more
responsibility.

God, I don't want to raise myself up. Help me to be
willing to work hard at whatever tasks I have and to
serve others. Amen.

JOHN THE BAPTIST

John's clothes were woven from coarse camel hair, and he wore a leather belt around his waist. For food he ate locusts and wild honey. (Matthew 3:4, NLT)

John the Baptist was a well-known preacher in Bible times, and he was also Jesus' cousin. John was not interested in worldly things like fancy food and expensive clothes. Instead, he ate bugs and wore rough clothes. He was not trying to impress anyone.

Lots of people try to say that God wants to make you rich, but this isn't always true. He does want you to do your best, but lots of people in the Bible were not rich. John was Jesus' own cousin and he wasn't rich. Even Jesus wasn't rich. God provides for you depending on the calling he has on your life. That means he provides you what you need.

Don't be consumed with being wealthy or dressing fancy. Love the Lord and he will take care of the rest.

God, I don't want to worry about silly things like clothes. I trust you to take care of me! Amen.

TIMOTHY

*Paul went first to Derbe and then to Lystra,
where there was a young disciple named Timothy.
His mother was a Jewish believer, but his father
was a Greek. (Acts 16:1, NLT)*

Not every kid has parents who believe in God.
Timothy's mom was a Christian, but his father
was not. The important thing was that Timothy
became a Christian and, later, he became a very
important pastor in the New Testament. He was
actually very young when he became a pastor.

God doesn't judge you by what your parents
do because he knows that you are not your mom
or dad ... you are you. Having a relationship with
Jesus is personal. It is something you must decide
to do on your own. Your parents may or may not
believe in the Bible, but God still loves you and
is willing to use you. The important question is,
have *you* chosen to believe in and follow Jesus?

God, I want to know you personally. I can't control what
my parents do or the choices they make, but I want to
place myself in your hands. Amen.

JOHN

When Jesus saw his mother there, and the disciple whom he loved standing nearby, he said to his mother, "Dear woman, here is your son," and to the disciple, "Here is your mother." From that time on, this disciple took her into his home. (John 19:26-27, NIV)

John is the only disciple believed to have been at the cross when Jesus was crucified. John was special to Jesus. While Jesus was dying, he wanted to know that his mother would not be alone; he wanted her to be cared for. From the cross, Jesus gave that task to John, and the Bible says that John took Mary into his home.

John was also most likely the youngest of all the disciples, but Jesus knew he could trust John with the special task of caring for Mary. John is a hero because he immediately did this practical task for Jesus – and it was a long-term commitment. Are you willing to be committed to obey Jesus, no matter what? If he asks you to do something, he trusts you. Are you worthy of that trust?

Jesus, I want to obey you no matter what. Help me to serve you and do what you ask of me. Amen.

MARY

*Simeon blessed them and said to Mary, his mother:
"This child is destined to cause the falling and
rising of many in Israel, and to be a sign that
will be spoken against, so that the thoughts of
many hearts will be revealed." (Luke 2:34-35, NIV)*

Mary was chosen to be Jesus' mother, but it must have been scary for her at times. First, she had the responsibility to raise the Son of God! Then, she probably didn't know how it was all going to work out – that her son would have to die on the cross – but these words of Simeon let her know that, at some point, being Jesus' mother was going to be painful for her. But she trusted God.

You have people you love, don't you? It would be tough to imagine someone you care about being hurt. One of the hardest things in life is to trust God with those you love. You have to trust that God knows what he is doing. Like Mary, trust God to take care of your friends and family. He loves them even more than you do.

Father, I sometimes get scared about what might happen to my loved ones. Please take that fear away. Amen.

THREE WISE MEN

When it was time to leave, [the wise men]
returned to their own country by another route,
for God had warned them in a dream not
to return to Herod. (Matthew 2:12, NLT)

The three wise men did not know that King Herod wanted to kill the baby Jesus, but God did. So God warned the wise men in a dream not to go back to Herod. The wise men listened to God and, even though Herod had asked them to come back and tell him where they found the baby, the wise men disobeyed.

Sometimes, like Herod, people lie and only want to cause trouble. You shouldn't trust everyone. Many times your parents can help you know who to trust, but other times God can show you who is honest and who is not. When God gave them a warning, the wise men obeyed God rather than the king. Like them, listen to God. Let him guide you. When you wonder if you can trust someone, talk to God. Always obey him.

Lord, give me wisdom to know who to trust and who not to trust. Amen.

JOHN MARK

Get Mark and bring him with you, because he is helpful to me in my ministry. (2 Timothy 4:11, NIV)

John Mark had traveled with Paul and Barnabas, but then, in the middle of a trip, he left them to go back home. When Paul and Barnabas were getting ready to travel again, Paul did not want John Mark coming because he didn't trust him. Eventually, however, John Mark did end up working with Paul again. When Paul was writing this very last letter to Timothy from prison, he asked that Timothy bring Mark with him "because he is helpful to me in my ministry."

In fact, John Mark probably wrote the Gospel of Mark in the New Testament. John Mark made a big mistake, but he is a hero because he kept on trying and, eventually, he earned Paul's trust and served God well. Maybe you have made a mistake. Ask for forgiveness and then do your best. God will take care of the rest.

God, I have made people angry in the past. I ask that you will fix the problems and help us work things out. Amen.

JEREMIAH

Before I formed you in the womb I knew you, before you were born I set you apart; I appointed you as a prophet to the nations. (Jeremiah 1:5, NIV)

God told Jeremiah that he knew him even before he was born. Jeremiah became a mighty prophet of God. He spoke the words of God when others would not. Jeremiah was a pretty important guy, and God knew him and set him apart for this special task before he was even born.

What's really cool is that God knew you before you were born, too! In the book of Jeremiah it says that God has good plans for you and your life and not bad plans. You probably don't know what those plans are yet, but you don't have to worry about it. When the time is right, God will let you know his plans for you and he will guide you.

God, thank you for having good plans for my life. I don't even understand how it is that you knew me before I was born, but I believe that you have good things in store for my life. Amen.

NEHEMIAH

I said to [the officials in Jerusalem], "You see the trouble we are in: Jerusalem lies in ruins, and its gates have been burned with fire. Come, let us rebuild the wall of Jerusalem." (Nehemiah 2:17, NIV)

Nehemiah wasn't a preacher and he wasn't a prophet. In fact, when Nehemiah heard about the broken-down walls of Jerusalem, he was in another country serving the king as a cupbearer. But he asked the king if he could go and help his people rebuild the walls of his city that had been destroyed by their enemies. A city without walls was open to invasion, and Nehemiah knew that the people needed a wall in order to be safe.

So Nehemiah went to the city, made a plan, and encouraged the people to rebuild the wall. Nehemiah is a good example that you don't have to speak from a pulpit to make a difference for God. Nehemiah was a good and fair leader, and he got the job done. Ask God to show you what he wants you to do for him.

Father, no matter what I do, I want to do it well for you. Make me like Nehemiah. Amen.

SOLOMON

David sent for his son Solomon and instructed him to build a Temple for the L<small>ORD</small>, the God of Israel. "My son, I wanted to build a Temple to honor the name of the L<small>ORD</small> my God," David told him. (1 Chronicles 22:6-7, NLT)

David called for his son Solomon and told him some important things that he would need to do when he became king. David wanted to build the temple for God in Jerusalem, but God said that his son Solomon should build it. So David spent many years gathering materials and making plans. David then passed the task on to his son, and Solomon completed it. Solomon is a hero for taking on the task from his father and completing it to the best of his ability. He knew that God would help him.

As you grow older, you will have many tasks to do in life. It is important to remember to honor your parents. If you have tasks to do today, be sure to do them with all your might.

God, help me to honor my parents. And when they trust me with important tasks, help me to do my best. Amen.

JONATHAN

Jonathan had David reaffirm his oath out of love for him, because he loved him as he loved himself. (1 Samuel 20:17, NIV)

Everyone knows that David killed Goliath. They also know that David became a great king. But many don't know that David would probably have been killed had it not been for his best friend Jonathan. King Saul was Jonathan's father, and Saul was jealous of David and wanted him killed. However, Jonathan loved David like a brother and helped keep David safe. Imagine what a friend that was, because Jonathan was the prince and would have been next in line to be king. But he supported and protected his friend David, who he knew would one day be king.

Jealousy can cause problems between people and it can hurt your friendships. Jonathan is a hero because he didn't let jealousy get in the way of his friendship with David. Instead, he was a true friend. How can you be a true friend?

Lord, help me to be a true friend. Amen.

ENOCH

It was by faith that Enoch was taken up to heaven without dying – "he disappeared because God took him." For before he was taken up, he was known as a person who pleased God. (Hebrews 11:5, NLT)

Enoch is not nearly as famous as other people in the Bible because not much is written about him. The Bible does say that he was so close to God that he never died – God simply took him right to heaven. A lot of people only worry about what happens in this life, but Enoch knew that the most important thing in life was to please God. Apparently he did a pretty good job, because he was known as a person who pleased God.

What do people know about you? What would your friends say is most important to you? Would it be all your stuff? Or would they say that the most important thing about you is that you are a person who pleases God?

God, I don't want to be concerned about stuff on earth more than you. Show me how to become known as a person who pleases you. Amen.

JULY

TAKE IT TO THE BANK (PROMISES OF GOD)

YOU ARE ROYALTY

Yet to all who received him, to those who believed in his name, he gave the right to become children of God. (John 1:12, NIV)

Have you ever dreamed of being a famous athlete or a movie star? Or perhaps a superhero or a warrior? Guess what? You can be royalty! That's right. Believing on God automatically makes you a child of God, which means you are royal. God is the King of all kings, and you can't get any higher than that. You are a son of God, a prince, in the biggest kingdom in the entire universe.

You won't be waited on hand and foot as royalty, but you most certainly benefit from being a child of God because God, your Father, watches over you. Now you can hold your head up high, knowing you are a child of the King. You are royalty.

Father God, I receive you into my life and I believe in the name of Jesus your Son. Thank you for making me your child and bringing me into your kingdom. Amen.

WHEN YOU GIVE, YOU RECEIVE

Give, and you will receive. Your gift will return to you in full – pressed down, shaken together to make room for more, running over, and poured into your lap. The amount you give will determine the amount you get back. (Luke 6:38, NLT)

There are many different ways to give. You can give a helping hand, give your best at school, give a nice card, give a donation, or give a hug. And even if you think your gift is small, it may have a big impact.

In all the ways you choose to give, don't do it just so you can get something back. That's not what giving is about. If you are giving just to *get*, you probably won't *get* what you were expecting.

God promises to reward you when you give, but be sure to bless others because it's the right thing to do. It always feels great and satisfying. You never know how it will come back. You may be surprised!

Lord, show me how I can give every day. I want your blessings in my life. Help me to be a blessing. Amen.

HELP IN TIMES OF TROUBLE

*God is our refuge and strength, an ever-present
help in trouble. (Psalm 46:1, NIV)*

In war, there are many, many stories of soldiers
who helped their buddies when they were in
trouble. Soldiers do their very best to help each
other, protect each other, and look out for each
other. But soldiers can only do so much. They
can't be everywhere at once and can't always get
to a fellow soldier in time.

God promises that he will be a refuge and
strength, someone who is always with you in
times of trouble. He is always there when you
need him, when you're afraid, when you're in
trouble, or even when you just want to talk to
him. He never ever leaves. God is always with
you.

God, you are my refuge and strength. I trust you. Thank
you that I can depend on you when I need help. Amen.

SAFETY

I will lie down and sleep in peace, for you alone,
O Lord, make me dwell in safety. (Psalm 4:8, NIV)

Jack had a hard time sleeping at night. He thought the boogie man was under his bed and that there were monsters in his closet. He was too afraid to look, so one night he asked his dad to look for him. His father said, "Son, come with me." His dad went into Jack's bedroom. Jack waited at the door while his dad looked. Then his father said, "It's Ok, Son, look." His dad showed him under the bed – no boogie man. Then he showed him in the closet – no monsters. "You see, Son, I wouldn't let you sleep in a room with monsters or the boogie man."

That's what your Father God promises to you – safety. Sleep in peace. God is with you.

Thank you, Lord, for keeping me safe. Please keep your angels at watch over me while I sleep. Amen.

ALWAYS WITH YOU

Never will I leave you; never will
I forsake you. (Hebrews 13:5, NIV)

The school bully told Joe he was going to beat him up after school. Joe looked at his friends and they all shook their heads saying, "Good luck, Buddy." Joe pleaded with his friends, "Come on guys. One of you has just *got* to go with me!" But none of his friends would go with him. However, his math teacher, Mr. Jones, said he would. When Joe showed up with Mr. Jones, the bully left him alone.

Whatever situation you are in, God promises to stick with you. He is always there for you. You can never be alone, because God promises to never leave or forsake you.

Dear God, please help me to remember that you will never leave me in times of trouble or in times of joy. Amen.

STRENGTH

*He gives power to the weak and strength
to the powerless. (Isaiah 40:29, NLT)*

There once was a superhero named Tad. He was just an average kid. He wasn't very big and was sometimes a little shy, but anytime someone was in trouble, Tad wanted to help. When help was needed, he would stick up his arms and say, "Poof!" And just like that, big muscles would appear along with super speed and energy. Eventually, the super powers wore off until the next time he needed them.

God promises you super strength, too! You can't say, "Poof!" and get big muscles like Tad, but when you feel like you can't handle a situation and you are tired of facing a problem, call on God. He promises to give power to the weak and strength to the powerless. He will give you the power and strength you need.

Dear God, I am so grateful for your promise of strength and power when I am in need. Amen.

COURAGE

*God did not give us a spirit of timidity,
but a spirit of power, of love and of
self-discipline. (2 Timothy 1:7, NIV)*

The Cowardly Lion wanted courage, so he went with Dorothy to see the Wizard in the Land of Oz. He hoped that the Wizard could give him courage. He finally was able to see the Wizard, who told him that he already had been courageous. The Lion didn't realize that he already had what it takes to be courageous. He didn't need magic from a wizard; he just needed to recognize what had been inside him all the time.

If you are a child of God, then you have the courage you need for any situation. When you start to fear, remember that your fear is not from God. He has promised you power, love, and self-discipline.

God, thank you for your good gifts of power, love, and self-discipline. I will stand on your promises when I am afraid. Amen.

ETERNAL LIFE

*I tell you the truth, he who believes
has everlasting life. (John 6:47, NIV)*

If someone promised that you could live forever, you might wonder what you would have to give up in return. What if you found out that the gift was free?

The gift of eternal life is promised to those who believe in Jesus Christ. That means living forever with Jesus in heaven. Your body will die, but you don't have to be afraid of that because your spirit will continue to live on. Jesus said that you will get a heavenly body (1 Corinthians 15:53) and you will live forever with no sadness or pain. Wow! What a promise!

Father God, I believe in you. You are my Lord and Savior.
I accept your gift of eternal life with you. Amen.

SECURITY

I give them eternal life, and they will never perish. No one will snatch them away from me. (John 10:28, NLT)

When you asked Jesus Christ into your life and believed on him, you became "snatch proof." That's right – snatch proof. You can rest assured that nothing and no one can ever take you away from God. Absolutely nothing! He wouldn't let that happen. He has given you the gift of eternal life so you can live forever with him.

You don't have to worry or stress out wondering if you will be with Jesus or not. He promised, and God *never* breaks a promise. Never! So relax. Jesus died to save you. He isn't going to let you go. You can feel secure in God's promise.

Jesus Christ, I am so glad that I belong to you and that no one can take me away from you. I love you! Amen.

GUIDANCE

The Lord says, "I will guide you along the best pathway for your life. I will advise you and watch over you." (Psalm 32:8, NLT)

Imagine you have just been placed in the middle of a forest. You have never been there before so you don't know your way around. There is nothing in the forest except you and nature. Now, try to find your way home. You look all around you and see several pathways. There are no signs indicating where the paths lead. Which one do you take? Which one leads home?

Life can be like that sometimes. It can be hard to make decisions about all sorts of things. You may even be worried that you might make a mistake. You were not put in life without direction or guidance. God will help you make the right decisions and guide you on the right path in life.

Lord, I need your direction and guidance in my life. I want to make the right decisions. I know you have the best path for my life. Help me to follow you. Amen.

ANSWERS TO PRAYER

You can pray for anything, and if you have faith, you will receive it. (Matthew 21:22, NLT)

First Kings 18 tells the story of how Elijah the prophet was sent by God to Samaria with the message that rain would soon come. There was no sign of rain, but Elijah had faith that it was coming because the Lord said so. Elijah sent his servant seven times to see if there were clouds coming. Each time the servant reported that there was nothing. On the seventh time, the servant reported back that there was a little cloud. Sure enough, it soon rained. Faith is believing in what you can't see. You may not see the answer to your prayer right away, but keep having faith and you will receive it. Don't give up! Keep asking and trusting in God. He promises to answer.

God, thank you for your promise that I can talk to you about everything and not be afraid to ask you for anything. Amen.

GOD'S FAITHFULNESS

If we are unfaithful, he remains faithful, for he cannot deny who he is. (2 Timothy 2:13, NLT)

Sammy went every Saturday to visit his grandma. His mother wanted him to go because she worked Saturdays and could not be around if Sammy needed her. Sammy couldn't do things with his friends. One Saturday, his friends were going to a free movie and then get pizza! Sammy *really* wanted to go, but he reluctantly declined because he knew he had to keep his word to visit Grandma. It was a good thing he did! His grandma had fallen that day and was hurt very badly. Because Sammy was faithful, he helped save his grandma.

You can be faithful to help others because God is faithful to you. God is always faithful, no matter what, because that is who he is. There is no way that he cannot keep his word. You can count on it, so make sure others can count on you. Be faithful to others as God is faithful to you.

Father God, please help me to be a faithful person. I am so grateful that you will always be faithful. Amen.

LOVE ALWAYS

Give thanks to the Lord, for he is good; his love endures forever. (1 Chronicles 16:34, NIV)

Friends disappoint, parents aren't perfect, and classmates might not like you, but God promises to love you. Bad things happen in life sometimes. Maybe they have happened to you. You may feel alone or unloved. Jesus knows exactly how you feel. While he was on earth, he experienced all the same feelings you do. He knows what it's like to be made fun of, to be mocked, abandoned, and hurt.

But God loves you so much and his love will never go away; in fact, the Bible says that God *is* love. He is a really good God. He will always love you. And his love lasts forever.

Thank you, Lord, for your love that will last forever. You are a good God. Amen.

JOY

The joy of the Lord is your strength.
(Nehemiah 8:10, NIV)

If you have ever been in a pillow fight, you probably know what it's like to be knocked down. But of course you don't stay knocked down. You quickly jump back up and whack the other person with your pillow. The game continues back and forth and even though you get knocked down, you continue to get back up and whack your friend with the pillow because – well – it's just so much fun!

In a way, that's what the joy of the Lord does for you. Just like in a pillow fight, the excitement of a chance to get your opponent helps you jump back up. And joy is something you want to give back – just like a fun smack with a pillow. The joy of the Lord gives you strength whenever you need it. It helps you keep on going.

Lord, please give me your joy today. Amen.

GOD'S PRESENCE

Come near to God and he will come near to you. (James 4:8, NIV)

God gives us a simple but wonderful promise that if we come near to him, he will come near to us. When you call on God, he is there. When you want to tell him things, he is listening. When you are afraid, he is there with you. When you feel alone, he is your friend.

Get closer to God today. He has things he wants to tell you – good things. He is always talking to you. You don't need a telephone to get close to God. You don't need to take an airplane to get close to him. You just need to talk to him, read his word, and listen.

God, I know you are speaking to me. Help me to hear your voice. I come to you today. Amen.

BEYOND IMAGINATION

No eye has seen, no ear has heard, no mind has conceived what God has prepared for those who love him. (1 Corinthians 2:9, NIV)

Have you thought about what you want to be when you grow up, places you want to go, and things you want to do? Imagine the most amazing life that you think you could have or would want to have. Got it? Think big. Did you know that there is no way you could dream up something better than the plan God has for you? It's true. You have no idea of all the things God has prepared for your life if you love him. Not everything may go perfectly because people aren't perfect, but just you wait for what God has in store for your life! God promises that it will be amazing.

Father, I am glad that my life is in your hands. I do love you. Amen.

LONG LIFE

Honor your father and mother, as the Lord your God commanded you. Then you will live a long, full life in the land the Lord your God is giving you. (Deuteronomy 5:16, NLT)

There once was an "honor" key that went to a secret door. All those who honored their parents found this key. Those who used it could unlock a gate that led to the pathway of a life that pleased God. If they went down that pathway, they would find many wonderful treasures along the way. Everyone who went down that path didn't want it to end. When the path ended, each person was glad they had found the key and used it.

You use this key when you honor your parents. It's hard at times to listen to your parents. You may not even want to say good things about them sometimes, but remember the honor key. If you want to live a long fulfilling life, you must use that key. Even more important, it pleases God.

Lord, please help me to honor my parents even when I don't feel like it. I want to do what you have asked. I want to go down the right path. Amen.

EVERYTHING YOU NEED

Seek first his kingdom and his righteousness, and all these things will be given to you as well. (Matthew 6:33, NIV)

God doesn't want you to worry. He cares about the needs of the smallest creatures, and he loves and cares for you even more. God promises that he will give you everything you need. You don't have to worry about food or clothes or anything you and your family may need.

Remember that a *need* isn't a new video game or the latest designer basketball shoes. Sometimes you get blessed with those things, but your needs are things that are necessary for living – like food, clothes, shelter. God sees your every need and promises that, if you seek after him, he will take care of you.

Father God, I will seek after you and godly things. Thank you for taking care of all my needs. Amen.

MERCY

*God blesses those who are merciful, for they
will be shown mercy. (Matthew 5:7, NLT)*

Jesus told a story about a servant who owed a
debt to a king, but he could not pay it back. The
man pleaded, so the king showed mercy and forgave the debt. The servant then went to a fellow
servant who owed him a debt and demanded that
he pay it back. His fellow servant could not repay his debt, so the first servant threw him in jail.
The king found out what happened and called
his first servant back. The king said that since he
had shown mercy on him, he should have shown
mercy to his fellow servant. Then the king threw
him in jail until he could repay his debt (Matthew
18:23-30).

There may be a time when you want mercy,
so remember God's promise and show mercy to
others.

Jesus, please help me to be a kind and merciful person
because you have been kind and merciful to me. Amen.

A LISTENING EAR

We are confident that he hears us whenever we ask for anything that pleases him. (1 John 5:14, NLT)

Have you ever felt that no one listens to you or understands you? God promises that he always listens and understands. You can talk to God and ask him for things, too. God cares about the things that you care about. He is listening to the things you ask of him if you ask according to his will. That means that you aren't asking for things that would be wrong or would hurt others.

So don't ever feel like you are bugging God. He is never too busy to spend time with you. In fact, he would drop everything else he was doing just to hang out with you if you asked him to, because he always offers a listening ear when you need it.

Dear God, I am so thankful that you listen to me. Please hear my prayers and teach me how to ask according to your will. Amen.

PROTECTION

All who listen to me will live in peace,
untroubled by fear of harm. (Proverbs 1:33, NLT)

It's always a good feeling to know you're safe. Some people have security systems, alarms, or even bodyguards for protection and to feel safe. Who doesn't want to feel safe and secure?

There is a way you can always feel safe and secure. It's a security system that keeps out evil. There are some instructions that you must follow in order for it to work. Listen to the Lord. That means when you know that God wants you to be kind to your teacher, you should. When God wants you to listen to mom and dad, hop to it. When he says not to hang out with a boy who is a bad influence, stay away!

Listen to what God has to say. It could be that very thing that he is telling you that will keep you safe. When you listen to him, he will help you live in peace and keep you safe.

Lord, I want to listen to you because I love you and I want to be under your protection. Please help me to listen to you and follow your way today. Amen.

IT'S ALL GOOD

We know that God causes everything to work together for the good of those who love God and are called according to his purpose for them. (Romans 8:28, NLT)

Drew's soccer team lost the championship game by just one point. Even though Drew was upset, he didn't show it. As captain of the team, he knew he had to set a good example. And as a Christian, he knew he wanted to act as Jesus would act. So after the game, he encouraged his team members and pointed out the good plays that *had* happened. One of the players came up to him and asked to go to church with Drew. He wanted to know Drew's God better.

God will work in your life in ways you can't predict. God can take even the bad things that happen and turn them around for good. It might not be what you expect, but God promises that he can work all things together for the good of those who love him.

God, I love you and trust you to turn bad things in my life into good things. Amen.

YOU'RE BRAND NEW!

Therefore, if anyone is in Christ, he is a new creation; the old has gone, the new has come! (2 Corinthians 5:17, NIV)

When you confess your sins to God, tell him you are sorry and ask for forgiveness, God will forgive. Then you can invite Jesus Christ to be the Lord of your life. At that very moment, the Bible says that you are a new creation – the Bible calls this being "born again." When you're born again, you don't become a baby; instead, your spirit is born again. That makes you a brand-new person. Being a new creation means that God has forgiven you. You are a child of God and he gives you a fresh start. You have Jesus in your life now. The old has gone, the new has come!

Father God, I am very sorry for all my sins. Please forgive me. I believe in your Son Jesus Christ and want to make you Lord of my life. Please come and live in me and make me a new creation. Thank you for a fresh start. Amen.

A PLACE IN HEAVEN

In my Father's house are many rooms; if it were not so, I would have told you. I am going there to prepare a place for you. (John 14:2, NIV)

It's so fun to dream about big houses, palaces, and mansions. Maybe you like to dream about all the cool things you would put inside a mansion. Well, you can stop dreaming. How would you like to live in the happiest place in the universe? It's a gazillion times better than you could ever dream up. It's a place of no more suffering, a place of joy, a place where you will live with Jesus forever.

When Jesus left the earth to return to heaven, he said that he was going to prepare a place for us. He didn't mean like at a hotel or at your grandma's. He meant a place where we can stay forever! If Jesus is preparing a place for you, you can bet it's going to be really cool.

Jesus, I believe in you and am glad that I am going to be with you forever in heaven someday. Help me to share your love with others and bring along as many people as I can. Amen.

RICHES

My gifts are better than gold, even the purest gold, my wages better than sterling silver! (Proverbs 8:19, NLT)

You just found a treasure chest filled with gold coins and sterling silver. It's too heavy to carry and you don't want to leave your treasure, so you decide to stuff your pockets and come back. You can't imagine anything better than tons of gold and silver, so you intend to take as many trips as you need to until you get all of it home.

Well, even if you never find a treasure chest or a pot of gold, God promises you better gifts. He says they are better than the purest gold and the finest silver. Go for God's riches. They pay better and last forever – and you don't have to try to carry it all in your pockets!

Lord, I am looking forward to the gifts that you have for me. Amen.

ANSWERS TO PRAYER

*Again, I tell you that if two of you on earth agree
about anything you ask for, it will be done for you
by my Father in heaven. (Matthew 18:19, NIV)*

It's always nice to hear yes when you ask for something. Jesus wants you to be sure you know that
he is listening and that Father God will answer
your prayers. He said that when two people
agree about something and get together to pray,
God will answer. So grab a friend, a brother or
sister, or your mom or dad – and pray. Does your
family need help? Get the family together and
pray! Do you want your friend to ask Jesus into
his heart? Then grab a Christian friend and pray!
Do you know someone who is sick and needs to
be healed? Find a friend to pray with you for this
person. God says it will be done. What a privilege
and joy it is to pray and watch God's answers!

Jesus, thank you for your promise. I will agree with
Christian friends and family in prayer. Amen.

A WAY OUT OF TEMPTATION

The temptations in your life are no different from what others experience. And God is faithful. He will not allow the temptation to be more than you can stand. When you are tempted, he will show you a way out so that you can endure. (1 Corinthians 10:13, NLT)

Dan's friends were going to a movie that he knew he shouldn't see, but he didn't want to be made fun of by not going. Dan was stuck and he didn't know what to do. He quickly prayed, "God help me." Just then he remembered that if he didn't make it home before curfew, he wouldn't get his allowance. He told the guys that he had to get home or he wouldn't have money to go out with them next week. God was faithful to Dan. The temptation had not been too strong for Dan, and he had shown Dan a way out of the tempting situation. God promises to help you whenever you are tempted. When you feel tempted, call out to God. Ask him to show you the way out.

God, help me to stand strong against temptations that come my way. When I am tempted, show me the way out. Amen.

WISDOM

My son, if you accept my words and store up my commands within you ... then you will understand the fear of the Lord and find the knowledge of God. For the Lord gives wisdom, and from his mouth come knowledge and understanding. (Proverbs 2:1, 5-6, NIV)

Think about the wisest people you know. Do they seem to make good decisions? Do things seem to go right for them more often than not? Do they seem to be blessed by God? All those things you see in the wisest people you know can also be true for you. The wisdom that comes from God is the wisdom you want. God has told you all the things you need to know to be wise. They have been written down in the Bible. Do what God tells you in his word and don't stray from it. Believe and obey, and you will receive wisdom from God.

Lord, I know that I need wisdom as I grow up. I want the wisdom that you promise. Help me to find wisdom as I read your word and learn more about you. Amen.

A LIGHT

Your word is a lamp to my feet and a light for my path. (Psalm 119:105, NIV)

Bob needed to get some more firewood for the campfire. He went into the woods to get it. As it was getting dark, the trees blocked the moonlight. Bob couldn't see his way back. Fortunately, he had remembered to bring his flashlight. The little light from his flashlight kept him from stumbling over branches and rocks and helped him see the path that led back to the campsite.

The word of God is like a flashlight, but no batteries are required. When you don't know what to do or which way to go, the word of God will light the way. It keeps you from stumbling. God talks to you in many ways – when you pray, through others, and through the Bible. The word of God is a light that will never die. It will light the path ahead of you, guide you, and keep you from getting lost.

Dear God, thank you for your word that lights the path ahead of me. Help me to study and understand it. Amen.

POWER

For the word of God is alive and powerful. It is sharper than the sharpest two-edged sword, cutting between soul and spirit, between joint and marrow. It exposes our innermost thoughts and desires. (Hebrews 4:12, NLT)

Ironman has a suit that is a powerful weapon against bad guys. But the Bible is even better. It is the most powerful weapon that anyone could ever own. The Bible is not just some ancient book about God. The word of God is living. That means that it has real power and can affect your life today. It's like a sharp sword that cuts deep into your life, helping you consider your thoughts and desires, making you want to change in order to show your love for God.

God's promises in the Bible are still true today. So get your sword and keep it sharp! God wants to speak to you today!

God, I love your word. Thank you that I can read it today. Thank you that it is alive and powerful and can help me live my life better for you. Amen.

FORGIVENESS

*If we confess our sins, he is faithful and just
and will forgive us our sins and purify us
from all unrighteousness. (1 John 1:9, NIV)*

There once was a shirt that had a bad stain. No matter how hard the shirt tried, it couldn't get the stain out. It couldn't put itself in the wash. It couldn't put on stain remover. One day the owner of the shirt applied stain remover and put the shirt in the wash. When the owner pulled out the shirt, the stain was gone and it was clean.

Everyone sins and does things that are wrong. Sin leaves a stain on your life. No matter how hard you try, you cannot get rid of it yourself. Did you know that there is nothing you have ever done that God cannot forgive? Confess your sins and he will forgive you and wash you clean.

Jesus, I am sorry for _____ . Please forgive me. Wash me clean today. Amen.

AUGUST

WORKING OUT (SPIRITUAL STRENGTH)

HOW TO GET STRONG

*Their purpose is to teach people to live
disciplined and successful lives, to help them
do what is right, just, and fair. (Proverbs 1:3, NLT)*

To train your body, you work out and do some running or lift some weights. To train your mind, you go to school and learn about history, math, and English.

As you get older, it is important to work out and learn new things, but the most important area to get stronger in is your spiritual life. There are also ways to train your spirit to get stronger spiritually.

Prayer, reading your Bible, and learning to obey God are big ways to get stronger. All you need to get started is have a willing heart to grow in God.

God, I want to get stronger spiritually. Help me and teach me what I need to know. Amen.

FOCUSING ON GOD

*Let me understand the teaching of
your precepts; then I will meditate on
your wonders. (Psalm 119:27, NIV)*

You think about stuff, don't you? You dream of being a sports hero or you wonder about that girl in science class. You devote your mind and heart to all sorts of things throughout the day, but focusing on God is something that many people forget. Most days, it is so easy to get busy with school, friends, and church events that you can often forget to really think about God and his wonders.

If you want to focus on God, you must make it a priority. That doesn't mean you have to give up thinking about everything else; it means that even as you study your homework or think about the future, you are always remembering that God loves you and is ultimately in control.

God, help me to learn how to focus on you and to grow as one of your servants. Amen.

AVOIDING DISTRACTIONS

*When you see the tassels, you will remember
and obey all the commands of the Lord instead of
following your own desires and defiling yourselves,
as you are prone to do. (Numbers 15:39, NLT)*

The devil doesn't want you to focus on God at all, so he will try to get you to think about pretty much anything else. He is a master of distraction – getting you to follow your own desires. That's why it is so important for you to make time to focus on God and his promises for you.

God told the Israelites to sew tassels on their clothing to help them remember him. Every time they saw the tassels, they would think about God and remember his love for them. Think about what you can do to remind you of God every day. Maybe you can carry something special in your pocket or in your wallet. Whatever it is, use it to remind you constantly of your relationship with God and how he wants you to live. That will help you avoid getting distracted.

Lord, help me just to think about you and keep you in mind as I go about my day. Amen.

PRAYER

God knows how often I pray for you. Day and night I bring you and your needs in prayer to God, whom I serve with all my heart by spreading the Good News about his Son. (Romans 1:9, NLT)

You have most likely heard other people pray and have probably prayed yourself. It's important to remember that praying is not just something you do because you think you are supposed to, but because you want a relationship with God. If your friend Juan never talked to you and ignored you every time you tried to talk to him, you would probably get hurt or upset. After a while of not talking, you might not even be friends anymore. God is always your friend, but he might get hurt if you ignore him and forget to pray to him. Prayer is talking to God, so don't ignore him, because you wouldn't like it if you were ignored.

Lord, forgive me if I have ignored you. I want to be best friends, so let's talk a lot! Amen.

FASTING

Go and gather together all the Jews of Susa and fast for me. Do not eat or drink for three days, night or day. My maids and I will do the same. And then, though it is against the law, I will go in to see the king. If I must die, I must die. (Esther 4:16, NLT)

Esther's people, the Jews, were going to be killed because an evil man had made up lies about them. Queen Esther needed the king to help her prevent that from happening. But there was a law that if someone came before the king and the king refused to see that person, he or she would be killed. So Esther fasted for three days and asked the Jews in the city to do the same.

Fasting is when you don't eat so you can focus on praying about a special need. It is a way to show discipline and sacrifice to God. God did have favor on Esther and her people were saved. Since you're a growing boy, you should be careful about how often you fast. You should talk to your parents first. Fasting is a big step to following Jesus.

Lord, I am willing to sacrifice to honor you. Amen.

WHAT FASTING ISN'T

So after more fasting and prayer, the men laid their hands on them and sent them on their way. (Acts 13:3, NLT)

Although you don't eat when you fast, it doesn't mean that you just starve yourself. If you talk to your parents and they approve of you fasting, then make sure that you fast with a purpose. Have a goal in mind as to what you will be praying for during your fast.

Prayer should be a part of your fasting because it tells God why you are fasting. If you are praying for your family, or praying for your country, or even praying for a miracle, be sure that you know what you are focusing on in prayer. Fast with a purpose in mind.

Lord, if my parents say it's okay, then give me the strength to fast. Help me to focus on you. Amen.

TYPES OF FASTING

*On coming to the house, they saw the child.
Then they opened their treasures and presented
him with gifts of gold and of incense and
of myrrh. (Matthew 2:11, NIV)*

When the wise men came to see Jesus, they all gave gifts. One gave gold, another myrrh, and the third incense. These were very expensive gifts.

Fasting is giving to God also – and it is a kind of sacrifice. There are different types of fasting. Giving up food for a short time is the most common, but you can also give up other things for a while, too. Or you can stop doing something in order to spend that time focusing on God. Think of something that you like to do and ask yourself if you could give it up for a little while in order to spend more time with God. For a week, take the time that you used to spend doing that activity and pray and read your Bible instead.

God, please show me what you want me to give up as a sacrifice to you. I can't wait to spend more time with you. Amen.

STUDY

Work hard so you can present yourself to God and receive his approval. Be a good worker, one who does not need to be ashamed and who correctly explains the word of truth. (2 Timothy 2:15, NLT)

André told Brian that God didn't like him, but Brian told him he was wrong. Andre told him to prove it, but Brian couldn't. Brian wished he knew the Bible better so he could tell Andre what the Bible says about God and how much he loves people.

You probably study for school, but it is also important to study the Bible because it is the most important book you can read. Start to hunger to read the Bible now. Don't wait until you are older. When you know the Bible, then you know the truth directly from God. Even if you only have a few minutes, spend some time every day reading the Bible.

Lord, help me to hunger for the Bible. I know I should read the Bible, so help me to want to read and study it. Amen.

BEING SIMPLE

The LORD has told you what is good, and this is what he requires of you: to do what is right, to love mercy, and to walk humbly with your God. (Micah 6:8, NLT)

Douglas stood in front of two doors. One said "Enter," but the other one said "Stay Out." Douglas was curious, so he went into the door that said to stay out. He stepped into a maze and got confused. He couldn't get out.

Sometimes people think that being God's child is difficult and confusing, like being stuck in a maze. The problem is, they are making it more difficult than God does. God wants you to be simple in serving him. He told the people through his prophet Micah that basically what he wanted was for them to do right, to love mercy, and to walk humbly with him. If you can do those things, you'll be on the right path. It's really not that difficult!

Lord, show me how to simply walk with you by doing right, loving mercy, and walking humbly with you. Amen.

WHY SIMPLICITY IS IMPORTANT

The law of the LORD is perfect, reviving the soul. The statutes of the LORD are trustworthy, making wise the simple. (Psalm 19:7, NIV)

When Antoine was standing outside, all he heard was noise because there were lots of cars racing by, horns honking, and people yelling. It was so loud that he couldn't hear his mom calling for him down the street.

Sometimes life can get so "noisy" that you can't hear anything, not even God. This is why it's so important to make your life simpler. The simpler you make your life, the less noise there is that keeps you from hearing God's voice. If there weren't any cars or horns, or yelling people, Antoine would have heard his mom.

What things in your life are "noisy"? What is getting in your way of hearing God? Talk to your parents about what you can do to make your life simpler.

God, I want to hear you, so please lower the volume on anything that is distracting me! Amen.

ALONE WITH GOD

*[Jesus] went up into the hills by
himself to pray. (Mark 6:46, NLT)*

David's parents decided to go out to eat together.
David wanted to go, but his dad said that tonight
was "parents' night." David's mom and dad wanted to spend some time together. His dad told him
that one-on-one time was very important for a
marriage, so David understood. When you spend
time with someone alone, then you give that
person all of your attention.

God wants to spend time with you all by
yourself. You go to church and worship him with
everyone else, but he also wants you to be one
on one with him. Where can you go to be alone
so that you can give God all of your attention?
If even Jesus needed time alone with his Father,
then so do you.

God, give me a bigger desire to spend time with you
alone. Amen.

ALONE TIME WITH GOD

[Elisha] went in alone and shut the door behind him and prayed to the Lord. (2 Kings 4:33, NLT)

You would probably be pretty bummed if you couldn't ever hang out with your parents. What if they didn't want to spend time with you by yourself? What if they only talked to you when there were twenty other people in the room? You probably wouldn't feel very important.

God is the same way. He wants to be the most important person in your life. When you and he spend time together, he has all of your attention. Elisha had an important request for God, and so he went alone into a room, shut the door behind him, and prayed. Being alone with God is important. Spend time alone with him.

Father, help me to remember how cool it is to be able to spend time with you. So many don't even know they can. Amen.

SUBMISSION

*Submit to one another out of reverence
for Christ. (Ephesians 5:21, NIV)*

In the military, soldiers obey orders from superior officers. Soldiers understand the importance of submission. Submission means that you obey someone who is in authority over you. Your leaders might be your parents, teachers, or pastor. God believes in submission because it's how you learn. When you submit, God rewards you. Sometimes it can be difficult to submit; you want to be grown up and not have to do what other people tell you to do. But God wants you to submit because you love Jesus. Don't be angry at those in leadership over you. Learn as much as you can from them. This honors God.

Jesus, help me to get better at listening to my leaders. I know it's the right thing to do, but it's not the easiest. Amen.

WHY SUBMISSION IS IMPORTANT

Since we respected our earthly fathers who disciplined us, shouldn't we submit even more to the discipline of the Father of our spirits, and live forever? (Hebrews 12:9, NLT)

Ten boys were stuck in a hole with enough wood and tools to build a ladder so they could get out. However, no one would listen to anyone else. The boys just argued and so they never built anything. They just stayed stuck in that hole. When there is no leader, then there is craziness because everyone has different ideas how to get something done. When there is a leader, everyone can follow the directions of one person. They can work together and get the job done.

God gave you parents so you would know who to listen to. Respect and obey your parents. This also teaches you how to respect and obey God.

Lord, I know that I need to listen to those who are my leaders, so give me a submissive heart to listen to you, to my parents, and to others who are in authority over me. Amen.

WHY SUBMISSION IS TOUGH

Since they did not know the righteousness that comes from God and sought to establish their own, they did not submit to God's righteousness. (Romans 10:3, NIV)

Submitting to someone else is often tough. One reason is because you want to be your own leader and you don't want to listen to anyone. Lots of kids feel like this as they grow up, but God doesn't like that kind of attitude.

When you only want to do what you want to do, that is a rebellious attitude and God does not like rebellion. If you don't submit to your parents, teachers, or pastors, then you are refusing to submit to God, too. Submission to your leaders is important because it helps show how submitted to God you are.

Lord, fix my attitude if you need to. I want my way sometimes, even though I know that's not right. Help me to submit when I should. Amen.

SERVICE

You, my brothers, were called to be free. But do not use your freedom to indulge the sinful nature; rather, serve one another in love. (Galatians 5:13, NIV)

Jesus was the Son of God, but he washed the feet of his disciples. This was before good sneakers, so the feet Jesus washed were probably very dirty and smelly. When people in Bible times walked on dusty, muddy roads in sandals, their feet got very dirty, so washing their feet was probably not a fun thing to do. Even though he deserved to be served, Jesus served those he led because he wanted to be an example to them.

Service is a sign of humility. It shows you aren't prideful and arrogant, but are willing to help other people out. Look around. Sometimes it just takes being aware of when someone could use your help. Take the initiative. Offer to help out and serve. This makes you like Jesus.

Jesus, even if I don't like to serve others, please help me to want to serve others. Help me to see where I can help others. Amen.

WHY SERVING IS IMPORTANT

Be shepherds of God's flock that is under your care, serving as overseers – not because you must, but because you are willing, as God wants you to be; not greedy for money, but eager to serve. (1 Peter 5:2, NIV)

A king was getting very old and he needed someone to take over from him when he died. He called together all of the men in his town and told them he needed a king to take over his job. He said he was looking for someone who could lead fairly and honestly. Each man told the king why he would be the best choice. Later, as the king was trying to decide who to choose, he saw one of the men helping an old lady walk across the street. The king picked that man because a good leader should serve the people he leads. When you serve others, you show that your heart has been touched by God. Lots of people want to be the star of the show, but few want to do the dirty work of serving. But even Jesus did that. He came to serve. He is your example.

Lord, help me to serve you in the little things. They don't seem important, but I know they are. Amen.

WHAT SERVICE ISN'T

But when you give to someone in need, don't let your left hand know what your right hand is doing. Give your gifts in private, and your Father, who sees everything, will reward you. (Matthew 6:3-4, NLT)

There was a turtle race that came down to two turtles that were racing for first place. But the race came to a stop because the judges realized that one of the turtles wasn't a turtle at all. It was a lizard that had glued a shell to his back to look like a turtle.

Sometimes people aren't what they look like either. Sometimes people pretend to serve others so they look good. You might not be able to tell, but God can see those who have the right hearts and those who are only serving because they want to look more spiritual. Serving others is not so you can look good; it's so that you humble yourself so others can see God's love in your heart.

Lord, help me to have good motives when I serve. I want to please you and not make myself look important. Amen.

CONFESSION

Therefore confess your sins to each other and pray for each other so that you may be healed. (James 5:16, NIV)

After Peter denied Jesus, he felt really bad about it. When he saw Jesus again, he confessed his sins and Jesus forgave him. Confessing is telling someone else the things you have done wrong. Confessing your sins might not always be easy for you, but it is really important that you be willing to do it. When Peter confessed his sins, Jesus was then able to forgive him. When you confess, it's like being able to start all over again because you don't have to carry around the weight of all your sins.

Everyone makes mistakes, so everyone needs to confess at some point. When we confess our sins to each other and pray for each other, we experience health and healing.

Lord, please forgive me of all my mistakes. Help me to be able to tell others the mistakes I have made even when I am embarrassed. Amen.

WHY CONFESSION IS IMPORTANT

If we confess our sins, he is faithful and just and will forgive us our sins and purify us from all unrighteousness. (1 John 1:9, NIV)

Luke saw Nelson break the car window, but Nelson made him promise not to tell anyone. Luke wanted to tell his mom, but was afraid he would get in trouble for being with Nelson. It bothered him so much he started to feel sick, so finally he told his mom the truth. She was glad that he told her the truth and Luke felt so much better.

When you confess your mistakes, you give God the chance to forgive you, but you also help yourself to feel better since you're not carrying around all the guilt. Confession might seem scary, but it's actually better than hiding everything.

God, I don't want to hide anything. I want to be able to be honest and open, so please show me how to do that. Amen.

WHO TO CONFESS TO

*O Lord, we acknowledge our wickedness and
the guilt of our fathers; we have indeed sinned
against you. (Jeremiah 14:20, NIV)*

Mason stole Vince's bike and then lied about
it. His parents found out and they made him
apologize to Vince, Vince's parents, their teacher,
and then to God.

When you need to confess, you should know
who to say you're sorry to. First, always tell God
you're sorry. Then, you need to confess and apologize to anyone who got hurt by what you did.
Confessing your sins might be the toughest of
spiritual disciplines because it means sharing a
secret. It also means that you have to admit being
wrong, which is always very difficult. God likes it
when we "come clean" with him and with others.
It gives us a clean slate and lets us start over.

Lord, give me a willingness to confess my sins and
wisdom to know how and when to do it. Amen.

WORSHIP

You must worship Christ as Lord of your life.
And if someone asks about your Christian hope,
always be ready to explain it. (1 Peter 3:15, NLT)

God is so awesome! He made the entire galaxy
and everything in it. He made every animal and
plant. He made the sun, moon, and all the stars.

He isn't just strong and creative, but he also
allowed his own Son to die so you could be saved.
That means he thinks you are worth saving. Because of all this, he deserves your worship. When
you worship, your focus and attention should be
on God and nothing else. Worship shouldn't be
tough. If you don't know how to start, begin by
telling God how much you love him. Then imagine hugging him and him hugging you back.

Jesus, I want to give you a great big hug and never let
go. Amen.

WHAT WORSHIP ISN'T

The Lord says: "These people come near to me with their mouth and honor me with their lips, but their hearts are far from me. Their worship of me is made up only of rules taught by men." (Isaiah 29:13, NIV)

Samuel was told that he needed to lift weights if he was going to get stronger, so he lifted weights over and over again for several months. However, Samuel did not get stronger. When his coach watched him work out, he realized that Samuel never lifted anything but the bar. He didn't put on any weight. The coach explained to him that simply going through the motions of lifting a bar does not make you stronger; he actually had to put weights on the bar to do that. Worship is not just a routine you do; it's not just speaking words or singing songs. Worship isn't worship unless your heart is drawing closer to God.

Lord, I don't want to go through the motions. I want my heart to be your heart. Amen.

GUIDANCE

This is what the LORD says: "Stand at the crossroads and look; ask for the ancient paths, ask where the good way is, and walk in it, and you will find rest for your souls." (Jeremiah 6:16, NIV)

Rick was about to kick the ball in order to score a goal, but his coach was yelling at him to kick it to Simon who was wide open and unguarded. Rick didn't hear his coach, so he kicked the ball at the net, but the goalie saved it. If Rick had heard his coach and followed his orders, then his team would have won the game. Those in authority help give you guidance.

There is no guidance more important than guidance from God. He is like Rick's coach. He is always looking out for you and trying to help you in your life. You simply have to listen. He will show you the path to follow. He will help you know what to do.

Jesus, I want to hear your voice and listen to your guidance. Show me the way! Amen.

WHY GUIDANCE IS IMPORTANT

*So today when I came to the spring, I prayed this prayer:
"O LORD, God of my master, Abraham, please give me
success on this mission." (Genesis 24:42, NLT)*

Ivan walked into the funhouse at the carnival, but
he got turned around and couldn't find his way
out. He found himself in the middle of a mirror
maze, so every direction looked the same. He kept
bumping into the mirrors because he couldn't tell
which way was the way out.

When you don't have the guidance of the
Lord, it is easy to get lost and confused. But when
God guides you, he will help your plans succeed.
Like Abraham's servant, you can pray for success
and then follow God's guidance. Only then will
your steps be secure and you'll find your way.

Jesus, I know when I follow you that I am going in the
right direction. Help me to know right away if I step off
the right path. Amen.

GUIDED BY GOD

*Follow my example, as I follow the example
of Christ. (1 Corinthians 11:1, NIV)*

Tom and his friends got lost in the woods. No one knew how to get back to camp, but Tom knew that the camp was at the north side of the park by the river. He also knew that moss always grows on the north side of trees. Tom began looking at the moss on the trees in order to figure out which way was north. Then he began to walk north in hopes of finding the camp. The other kids followed him because he seemed to know which way to go.

When you are led by God in your everyday life, other people will take notice. If you set a good example, people will look to you as a role model. Leading others isn't as hard when you are being guided by God.

Lord, please guide me and be a good example to those who follow me. Amen.

CELEBRATION

Nehemiah continued, "Go and celebrate with a feast of rich foods and sweet drinks, and share gifts of food with people who have nothing prepared. This is a sacred day before our Lord. Don't be dejected and sad, for the joy of the LORD is your strength!" (Nehemiah 8:10, NLT)

When Greg got good grades on his report card, his whole family went out to eat to celebrate his hard work. God doesn't want his people to be serious and boring all the time. When something great happens, he wants you to celebrate. In the Old Testament, God told his people to hold many celebrations at different times of the year. And when the people of Israel finished building the wall around Jerusalem, Nehemiah said they should celebrate just as God had told them in his word.

When God blesses you or your family, then take the time to celebrate and thank him! God loves it when you joyfully celebrate him!

Jesus, thank you so much for everything. Help me to be the best celebrator ever, but let my celebrations be pleasing to you. Amen.

WHY CELEBRATING IS IMPORTANT

The master said, "Well done, my good and faithful servant. Let's celebrate together!" (Matthew 25:23, NLT)

Kevin was not feeling well, but he wasn't sick. He felt bad because he was doing poorly in school, his family was moving in a few weeks to a new city, and he was going to miss his friends. It wasn't the best time of Kevin's life. When he got home from school, he discovered that there was a going-away party for him. All of his friends were there. They had lots of fun. Kevin would miss his friends when he moved, but he would always remember them. Life can sometimes be tough, but God gives you special celebrations as things to look forward to. You should always celebrate God and his love for you, but sometimes he gives you special moments to encourage and uplift you. Enjoy those special times, but celebrate God's greatness all the time.

Lord, thank you so much for all of the good moments in my life. Amen.

WHAT CELEBRATING ISN'T

Let us celebrate the festival, not with the old bread of wickedness and evil, but with the new bread of sincerity and truth. (1 Corinthians 5:8, NLT)

Aiden was so fast that he beat everyone in his school when they raced against him. But when he won, he was mean. He always told them how much better he was than them and how slow they all were compared to him. No one wanted to be Aiden's friend because he made them feel small.

That's not what celebrating is about. And when you celebrate God, you don't have to feel small in order to make him big. God is already big and powerful and wonderful. You celebrate him when you recognize him for who he is and you give him your sincere and true love. When you celebrate God, your joy should draw people to him because they want to be happy like you.

God, you are so big and amazing and wonderful. I celebrate you because I love you! Amen.

KEEP WORKING OUT

Since we are surrounded by such a huge crowd of witnesses to the life of faith, let us strip off every weight that slows us down, especially the sin that so easily trips us up. And let us run with endurance the race God has set before us. (Hebrews 12:1, NLT)

All of these spiritual lessons help you to grow with God. Prayer, fasting, studying, and all of the others give you strength, but you have to keep doing them to stay strong. It's like running a race. The more you run, the farther you can go. If you stop running, you lose your endurance. It's the same in school, too. If you stop studying, your grades get worse. God loves you no matter what, but if you want to stay as close to him as possible, then don't stop praying and learning about him. God looks forward to you spending time with him, so keep up the good work.

Lord, I want to be spiritually strong. I know others want big muscles, but more than anything I want you in my life. Amen.

STRENGTH IN NUMBERS

Where two or three gather together as my followers,
I am there among them. (Matthew 18:20, NLT)

If you take a pencil and try to break it, then you probably could. It isn't that hard to break one pencil. If you add another pencil and try to break them both at the same time, it gets a little harder. If you add even one more pencil, then it's almost impossible.

Getting spiritually stronger is just like that. You are stronger when you are with others who want to be close to God, too. Jesus said that when two or three gather in his name, he's right there among them. You can't get much stronger than that! So ask your friends and parents to pray, fast, and study with you so you all grow together. There is strength in numbers.

God, please give me people I can grow with. Amen.

SEPTEMBER

PEOPLE ISSUES
(PRACTICAL BIBLE ADVICE)

SHARING

*So the people went away to eat and drink at a
festive meal, to share gifts of food, and to celebrate
with great joy because they had heard God's words
and understood them. (Nehemiah 8:12, NLT)*

Jake's little sister was very selfish. She would go
around grabbing everything and yell, "Mine!" even
if it wasn't hers. She was just a little kid, but she
did not like to share. When they are very young,
most kids are selfish. They have to be taught to
share with others.

Jesus came to earth to show everyone how to
live and treat people, just like your parents show
you how to treat people, too. If you want to be
a good friend, you must learn to share, because
people don't like to hang around selfish people.
To be a good example of God to others, you
should share. After all, God isn't selfish – he gave
his Son for you.

God, I know it's important to share with others. Please
touch my heart so I will be more willing to share. Amen.

DON'T GOSSIP

A troublemaker plants seeds of strife; gossip separates the best of friends. (Proverbs 16:28, NLT)

Nathan liked to talk about people. If he knew someone's secrets or heard a rumor, then he would tell it to other people. It was his way of getting people to pay attention to him so he could feel important. It didn't matter if what he passed along was true or not; in fact, he didn't care at all. Before long Nathan had spread secrets about everyone in town, so no one liked him. He had hurt pretty much all of the people he knew. Nathan was very lonely, because eventually no one would talk to him for fear of him passing along what they said, and no one wanted to listen to his gossip.

Gossiping about people is one of the things God dislikes. As the Bible says, it will soon separate you from your friends. There are plenty of other things to talk about – so don't gossip. It will only hurt you in the long run.

God, help me to keep my mouth shut about other people and not to gossip. Amen.

DON'T LISTEN TO GOSSIP

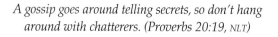

A gossip goes around telling secrets, so don't hang around with chatterers. (Proverbs 20:19, NLT)

Greg was Nathan's friend. He didn't gossip like Nathan, but he never stopped Nathan from gossiping either. Greg didn't like it when Nathan talked badly about people, but he didn't say anything. Because he hung out with Nathan, the other kids at school didn't like him either. Even though he didn't gossip, everyone saw Greg the same as Nathan.

The Bible says that not only should you not gossip, but that you shouldn't even hang around gossips either. Do any of your friends talk badly about anyone? If so, maybe you should tell them to stop. If your friend talks badly about another person, then he will probably talk badly about you, too.

Lord, give me the courage to tell other people to stop gossiping. I know it's the right thing to do, but it is not always the easiest thing to do. Amen.

CHOOSING FRIENDS

My friends scorn me, but I pour out my tears to God. (Job 16:20, NLT)

Bobby was popular and he hung out with the popular kids. All of them had lots of money because their parents had good jobs. When Bobby's dad lost his job, Bobby couldn't buy the nice things he used to and he couldn't go to the expensive places with his rich friends. He even had to sell his new car to pay for bills. Bobby's friends wouldn't hang out with him anymore because, to them, he was no longer cool. Bobby had not chosen very good friends, because good friends would have stuck with him in a difficult time.

You should be smart when you choose your friends. Don't hang out with people who only like you because you have money, or are the types of people who talk badly about other people. Choose friends who will stand by you if you go through a tough time. Even better, choose friends who also love Jesus!

Lord, I want friends I can trust. Please show me who is like that and give me good friends. Amen.

PICKING ON GIRLS

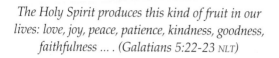

The Holy Spirit produces this kind of fruit in our lives: love, joy, peace, patience, kindness, goodness, faithfulness ... . (Galatians 5:22-23 NLT)

Ryan liked to pick on girls at school. He thought it was funny because the girls just didn't know how to take a joke. However, one day when he got home from school, Ryan saw his younger sister crying because boys at her school teased her. Ryan didn't like to see his sister cry, and he felt bad that he was just like the boys who made his sister cry. Girls and boys are both important and God loves them both equally, but they aren't the same.

In Genesis, the Bible says that God made women special. Don't be mean to girls. Instead, as a Christian, you should be an example to others and show the fruit of the Spirit by being kind and good to the girls you know.

Lord, help me to be more sensitive to girls. Grow the fruit of the Spirit in my life so that I show kindness and goodness to them. Amen.

FORGIVING

If you forgive those who sin against you, your heavenly Father will forgive you. (Matthew 6:14, NLT)

Rupert accidently broke his dad's tool, but his dad forgave him because it was just an accident. However, when Rupert's little brother broke his iPod, Rupert got angry and made him give him his allowance for breaking his favorite thing. Rupert's dad wasn't happy because Rupert was forgiven, but he would not forgive his brother.

God says in Matthew that God forgives you when you forgive those who have hurt you. So, if you want to be forgiven for your mistakes, forgive anyone who has done you wrong.

Jesus, help me to be able to forgive anyone who has done wrong to me. Thank you for forgiving me. Amen.

PEER PRESSURE

So at the sound of the musical instruments, all the people, whatever their race or nation or language, bowed to the ground and worshiped the gold statue that King Nebuchadnezzar had set up. (Daniel 3:7, NLT)

Chris saw that all the kids at his table in the lunchroom were putting peanut butter on their faces, but he thought it was weird. They all told him he should do it too, because everyone was doing it. So he did, even though he thought it was stupid, because he didn't want to be the only one not doing it. That's pretty silly, isn't it? But people often do really stupid things – things they know they shouldn't do – simply because the people around them are doing it and they don't want to be left out. In the book of Daniel, everyone was bowing to worship a statue as a god just because they were told to and just because everyone else was doing it. Peer pressure is when you feel like you have to do something because others tell you to. When you love God, you should do what is right – even if you are the only one.

Lord, help me to stand strong. Amen.

KEEPING A PROMISE

Remember your promise to me; it is
my only hope. (Psalm 119:49, NLT)

Jason's uncle promised him that he'd take him to a baseball game, but he never did. In fact, his uncle made many promises that he never kept, so Jason was hurt deeply. He used to look up to his uncle, but after so many lies, it was tough to trust him. Have you ever had someone promise you something, but the person didn't keep his word?

It doesn't feel good to be let down. God keeps all of his promises to you, and he wants you to keep your promises. If you want people to trust you, make sure you keep your word.

Lord, I want to be like you and keep my promises. Please remind me of the promises I make so I can be true to my word. Amen.

ENCOURAGE

We have different gifts, according to the grace given us. If a man's gift is ... encouraging, let him encourage ... . (Romans 12:6, 8, NIV)

Stephen thought he was dumb because everyone else told him he was. Mrs. Morrow didn't think that. She told Stephen he was very creative and good at coming up with ideas. With a little bit of encouragement from Mrs. Morrow, Stephen began to have more confidence. The Bible says that the words we speak to others have great power to help or to hurt. The apostle Paul even wrote about how some people have a special gift of encouragement. But you don't have to have that gift in order to be an encouragement to others. There are people who need to be encouraged, so tell them how much you appreciate them or point out how good they are at something. You know how good it feels when people encourage you, so be sure to do that for others.

Jesus, I want to be encouraging to those who need it. Show me who needs encouragement and help me to know what to say. Amen.

PATIENCE

Teach the older men to exercise self-control, to be worthy of respect, and to live wisely. They must have sound faith and be filled with love and patience. (Titus 2:2, NLT)

Aaron really wanted a new video game, but his mom told him to wait. Aaron had saved up money that he made by mowing lawns, so he bought the game anyway. That night was his birthday party and when Aaron opened up his gift from his grandpa, he realized why his mom told him to wait. His grandpa had gotten him the same game.

God wants you to have patience so you will be willing to wait on his timing. If you rush ahead of God, then you might mess things up. He knows what's best, so don't try to make everything happen now.

Lord, I know I like to have things right now, but help me to be patient and wait for your timing. Amen.

PRIDE

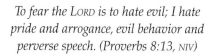

To fear the LORD is to hate evil; I hate pride and arrogance, evil behavior and perverse speech. (Proverbs 8:13, NIV)

Will thought he was the most amazing person who ever lived. Whenever someone complimented him, his head got a little bit bigger. Will thought he was better than everyone else. Eventually his head got as big as a hot air balloon and he floated away. At first, he thought that was fitting since he was higher than anyone else. It made him feel important. Then, one day, he realized he couldn't land. He just floated away and no one even missed him.

One of the biggest things that God dislikes is pride, because pride is thinking you are better than everyone else. Pride only points to you. God wants you to be humble, so through your humility people will be drawn to him.

Lord, I don't want my head to get full of pride. Help me to be humble, so I can be a good reflection of you. Amen.

COMPLAINING

Do everything without complaining or
arguing. (Philippians 2:14, NIV)

God freed the Israelites from slavery, but after a while of walking around in the desert they started complaining. God had provided food, water, and their freedom, and they still weren't happy. They should have been thankful, because God allowed them to cross the Red Sea and got them away from Pharaoh's army. But as they got tired and thirsty and hungry, they started to complain.

Do you ever complain? You might not have everything you want, but you have more than you would if God didn't help provide for you. The Bible says to do everything without complaining, so it's not okay to complain. Instead, remember all that God has done for you and be happy with what you have.

Jesus, please forgive me for my complaining. I know I am blessed to have what you have given me. Amen.

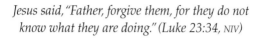

GOD'S LOVE

Jesus said, "Father, forgive them, for they do not know what they are doing." (Luke 23:34, NIV)

When Jesus was on the cross, people made fun of him. He could have been revengeful. He could have called down legions of angels to rescue him and take out the bad guys, but he didn't. Instead, even while suffering on the cross, he asked God to forgive them because they didn't know what they were doing. By not being hateful, Jesus was showing God's love.

As a Christian, the best way to tell your friends about God is to show them his kind of love. In every situation, ask yourself how Jesus would show his love, then do that and watch how people respond. Everyone needs love, but many kids your age don't get the love they need. So be a light by showing the love of God to everyone around you.

Jesus, help me to love like you want me to love. I know I don't know everything, but I am willing to learn. Amen.

PROTECTING OTHERS

Help him to defend the poor, to rescue the children of the needy, and to crush their oppressors. (Psalm 72:4, NLT)

God doesn't like it when the weak and poor get picked on. The Bible says to take care of orphans and widows, to help the poor and needy, and to seek justice against those who hurt others. It even warns against anyone making fun of the poor or homeless.

Has anyone ever protected you? Have you protected someone? You might be young and small, but you can still find ways to protect others. If you're at church or school and a bully is making fun of someone, stick up for the person and tell the bully to stop. If a bigger kid is picking on a smaller kid, you can tell an adult. Whatever you do, don't just watch. When you help others, you're on God's side – and he'll give you the courage you need.

Lord, give me courage to help others and wisdom to know what to say. Amen.

TOGETHER IN HEAVEN

The twelve gates were twelve pearls, each gate made of a single pearl. The great street of the city was of pure gold, like transparent glass. (Revelation 21:21, NIV)

As you get older, you will make many friends and you will have fun with family members, but sometimes you lose touch with people. Some move away and others die, but the great news is that every one of the people you know who is a Christian will be in heaven. Heaven is going to be a great place!

Can you imagine being able to see your friends and family there? Also, you will get to meet all of the great people mentioned in the Bible who loved God. And in heaven, you'll get to be with God forever. Don't get down about the bad things that happen on earth, because heaven is going to be great. If you are feeling down, think about how great heaven will be!

Lord, I am so excited about heaven. I know there are streets of gold and other cool things, but I am most excited about spending time with you. Amen.

LOVE YOURSELF

Love your neighbor as yourself. (Matthew 22:39, NIV)

Nick was very insecure because he wasn't very tall, strong, popular, or even smart. He felt that he was the least important kid on the planet and so he didn't like himself very much. Then Nick read in the Bible about how Jesus said that the greatest commandments are to love God completely and to love other people as much as you love yourself. Nick realized that he first had to love himself in order to love others.

Loving yourself doesn't mean becoming selfish and proud; it just means loving who you are because of how God created you. You are a child of God. That means you are important! If you feel low about yourself, then you aren't seeing yourself through God's eyes. When you see yourself as God sees you, then you can love yourself and that frees you up to love others.

Lord, help me to see myself through your eyes. Help me to love myself so that I can love others. Amen.

HONESTY

May integrity and honesty protect me, for
I put my hope in you. (Psalm 25:21, NLT)

In the old story of the boy who cried wolf, the young man kept lying about a wolf trying to get him. Every time he cried out, people came running to protect him, but there was never a wolf at all. But one day a wolf really did come, and when the boy cried wolf, no one believed him. No one came to help; he had lied so many times, the people figured he was lying again. The wolf ate the boy's entire flock of sheep. The point is that if you lie, people won't believe you when you actually do tell the truth. God felt so strongly about lying that he put it in the Ten Commandments that you shouldn't lie. Many places in the Bible talk about how much value God places on honesty. If you want your friends and parents to trust you, then make sure you are honest and avoid telling lies.

Lord, I want people to trust me, so help me to only tell the truth. Amen.

BEING A REAL FRIEND

There are "friends" who destroy each other, but a real friend sticks closer than a brother. (Proverbs 18:24, NLT)

When you are passionate about something, it means you like something so much you'd do almost anything for it. For example, some people are passionate about sports, books, gaming, and even TV.

Obviously, the most important thing to be passionate about should be God. However, God also wants you to be passionate in your relationships. He wants you to be a real friend to your friends – someone who cares passionately for them, who will stick by them, stick up for them, be there when they need you. If you have friends, then make sure you care about them. God loves it when he sees his people working together sharing his love with one another.

Jesus, help me to care about others as much as I care about myself. Help me to be a real friend. Amen.

PURITY

Create in me a pure heart, O God, and renew a steadfast spirit within me. (Psalm 51:10, NIV)

In many parts of the world, it snows during winter time. Clean, white snow is fun to play in. However, the snow doesn't stay white for long. In cities, the pollution from car exhausts makes the snow black and gross. Most people don't like to play in gross snow because it isn't pure anymore.

Something is pure when there is nothing bad in it – nothing there that shouldn't be, nothing dirty. To have a pure heart means to stay clean before God. When you sin, it makes your heart impure. To get it pure again, you need to confess and ask God to forgive you. Be pure in heart and obey God. Stay far away from sin.

Lord, help me to be pure in mind and in my heart. I know I'm not perfect, but I want to stay away from sin as much as I can. Amen.

COURAGE

As the time of King David's death approached, he gave this charge to his son Solomon: "I am going where everyone on earth must someday go. Take courage and be a man. Observe the requirements of the LORD your God, and follow all his ways." (1 Kings 2:1-3, NLT)

David was full of courage. He might be one of the bravest people in the entire Bible, so it is important to notice his last words to his son, Solomon. When David was about to die, he told his son to take courage. How was his son supposed to do that? David said that his son could have courage by observing God's laws, following his ways, and obeying him. He didn't say to get big and strong or to work out every day ... he told his son to obey God. Obeying God isn't always easy; it makes sense that this was how a man really shows that he has courage. You can show your courage by obeying what God has told you to do already in the Bible.

Father, help me to have courage and to do what you ask me to do. Amen.

CHURCH

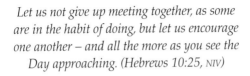

Let us not give up meeting together, as some are in the habit of doing, but let us encourage one another – and all the more as you see the Day approaching. (Hebrews 10:25, NIV)

When God made Adam, he said that it was not good for a man to be all alone, so he made Eve. Soon they had a family, and now there are lots and lots of people in towns and cities all over the world.

In the New Testament, the disciples started churches so Christians could learn more about Jesus and stay strong by encouraging each other. Sometimes when kids get a bit older, they forget how important going to church is. Whatever you do, don't forget that being involved in a local church is really important. It's never good for anyone to be all alone.

Lord, give me a deep desire to stay connected to a local church no matter how old I get. Amen.

NOT GIVING UP

Pursue righteousness and a godly life, along with faith, love, perseverance, and gentleness. (1 Timothy 6:11, NLT)

Thomas Edison invented the electric light bulb. Without his work, we would still be reading by candlelight, and there would be no TV or computers. However, Edison failed many times. It took him a long while to figure out exactly how to get his light bulb to work. Aren't you glad he didn't give up?

Sometimes life might not work out exactly how you want it to, but you must remember that there are times when you just have to keep on trying, even when it is hard. The apostle Paul encouraged his young friend Timothy to pursue perseverance, which means not to give up. That's good advice for you. Don't give up. The best things God has for you might just require a little bit of hard work.

Father, help me to not be a quitter. Even if I feel like giving up, please give me the strength to keep on trying. Amen.

ENJOY BEING YOUNG

Don't let anyone think less of you because you are young. Be an example to all believers in what you say, in the way you live, in your love, your faith, and your purity. (1 Timothy 4:12, NLT)

Zane always wanted to be older just like his brother Greg, but when Zane actually did grow up, he missed just being a kid. Most kids want to grow up as fast as they can, but a lot of adults wish they could go back to being kids. The point is that you should enjoy where you're at, because tomorrow will come soon enough. Youth is a fun time where you are still discovering new things. Even though you are young, you can still set an example for doing what is right. Don't be in a rush to grow up. Enjoy every day and take advantage of every opportunity you have now, but do it in ways that help you always show your love and commitment to God.

Lord, I often wish that I was older so I could do more things, but I do want to enjoy the time I have just being me. Amen.

PRIORITIES

Jesus replied, "The most important commandment is this: 'Listen, O Israel! The LORD our God is the one and only LORD. And you must love the LORD your God with all your heart, all your soul, all your mind, and all your strength.'" (Mark 12:29-30, NLT)

The pyramids in Egypt have a wide base and a pointy top. If the bottoms of the pyramids were pointy and the top were wide, then the pyramids would have fallen over because there would not be a strong enough base. For something to stand strong, it needs a solid foundation. In the same way, to build a strong life, you need a solid foundation.

You need to know what is the most important. In your life, the most important thing is to put God first. Sometimes guys try to make sports or video games their priorities, but those must not be the most important things in your life. Let God be your foundation so you can build a strong life.

Jesus, I want to build on a solid foundation. I want you to be the most important priority in my life. Amen.

SELF-CONTROL

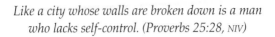

Like a city whose walls are broken down is a man who lacks self-control. (Proverbs 25:28, NIV)

Roller coasters are fun because they are exciting, but they are also safe. There are all sorts of rules in place to make sure nothing goes wrong. However, if the rules are ignored, then roller coasters would be very dangerous and scary. Would you want to ride a broken roller coaster? Those rules are in place to make sure the roller coasters don't go out of control and hurt people.

In the same way, God put rules in place so that you don't go out of control, but you have to have self-control to be able to follow the rules. Self-control is being able to keep yourself out of trouble. You would be like a roller coaster that didn't have protective rails or inspections. Every time you tell the truth, decide to do the right thing, and respect your parents, you show self-control. It might not always be easy, but it's far better than being out of control.

Lord, help me to have self-control so I don't do things I know wouldn't please you. Amen.

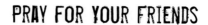

PRAY FOR YOUR FRIENDS

We always thank God, the Father of our Lord Jesus Christ, when we pray for you. (Colossians 1:3, NIV)

Great movies like *Star Wars* didn't have just one hero. A whole team of heroes worked together to save the galaxy. In real life, you also need help to live a godly life and be a light of God's love to the world. Your friends need you to pray for them, and you need them to pray for you as well. They are part of your team of heroes that is serving God in the world. Prayer is one of the most important parts of being a Christian, but it is often forgotten. Even if you can't help friends in other ways, you can help them a lot by praying for them.

Lord, please remind me to pray for my friends, so you can work in their lives. Amen.

DON'T BE A CHAMELEON

Don't copy the behavior and customs of this world, but let God transform you into a new person by changing the way you think. Then you will learn to know God's will for you, which is good and pleasing and perfect.
(Romans 12:2, NLT)

Chameleons change color so they blend into the land around them. This helps to protect them from predators because they can hide and not be seen. Sometimes people try to be like chameleons; they change what they say and believe depending on who they are with. The Bible says not to copy the behavior and customs of the world but to let God transform you – then you need to stand up and show it! If you really love Jesus, you can't hide it from other people. God doesn't want you to be like a chameleon. He wants you to stand out so other people can see how you live.

Jesus, help me to stand strong in what I believe, so that I don't change my mind over and over again. Amen.

BE A ROLE MODEL

You yourself must be an example to them by doing good works of every kind. Let everything you do reflect the integrity and seriousness of your teaching. (Titus 2:7, NLT)

A role model is someone you look up to and try to be like as much as you can. The best role model is Jesus because he was perfect. He is the only role model you can look to who never made a mistake. Jesus was a role model for you so that you can be a role model to others.

When you're at school or in your neighborhood, set an example of what Jesus was like to all the kids you know. Everyone needs a role model. Some of the kids you know might not know anything about Jesus, but by setting an example for them, you show them Jesus in your actions.

Jesus, help me to be a good role model, so I can share your love to my friends who don't know you. Amen.

BE RELIABLE

"Well done, my good servant!" his master replied. "Because you have been trustworthy in a very small matter, take charge of ten cities." (Luke 19:17, NIV)

Lance used to like walking to the old river bridge, but every time he tried to cross, one of the planks would break. Eventually it got too dangerous to cross the old bridge, so no one ever used it again. It wasn't reliable. Your relationships can be like old rickety bridges at times. If your friend can't rely on you, then your friendships won't last for long. In the same way, when you know you can't depend on people, you don't want to hang out with them.

Be a reliable friend. You show you are reliable by showing up when you say you will, being on time, keeping your promises, working hard, helping when it's needed, and telling the truth. If you do these things, you won't become unreliable like that old bridge.

Lord, help me to be reliable so my friends know they can trust me. I want to be trustworthy. Amen.

BE A FRIEND

The King will reply, "I tell you the truth, whatever you did for one of the least of these brothers of mine, you did for me." (Matthew 25:40, NIV)

Jesus is the King of all other kings, but he came to earth to be friends with anyone who was willing to be his friends and repent of his sins. Because you are a Christian, you are adopted into God's kingdom, so you too can be a friend to those who need friends.

Many kids in your school and neighborhood might not seem like they are lonely, but lots of them are. When you reach out to them and be their friend, you are doing what Jesus would want you to do. He says that being kind to people who need help is the same as being kind to him. Ask God to show you who needs a friend and then tell them about the best friend ever – Jesus!

Father, please show me those who need you as their friend. Help me to be a good friend to them, too. Amen.

OCTOBER

FIRST THINGS FIRST (PRAISE AND WORSHIP)

GOD DESERVES YOUR WORSHIP

Because of your unfailing love, I can enter your house; I will worship at your Temple with deepest awe. (Psalm 5:7, NLT)

When your favorite team wins the championship you cheer, don't you? Why? Because your team has beaten everyone else and deserves your applause. This is also why you should worship God. God is amazing and loves you no matter what, so he deserves your praise and worship. He doesn't have to love you, but he chooses to. It is okay to enjoy sporting events, but make sure you don't cheer on your team with more energy than you worship God.

God is way cooler than a sports game. God is stronger than a football or rugby player. He is faster than a sprinter, and he can jump higher than any basketball player. Worship God because he deserves your praise.

God, you are awesome! You deserve all of my praise. Amen.

WHAT WORSHIP IS

Then the Lord said to Moses, "Go back to Pharaoh and announce to him, 'This is what the Lord says: Let my people go, so they can worship me.'" (Exodus 8:1, NLT)

God thinks worship is important. So important that he freed all of the Israelites from slavery so they could worship him. You can worship God in a lot of ways, but you must submit yourself to be a servant of God to truly and honestly worship him.

In Exodus 8, the word "worship" means to serve. Mother Teresa is a great example of a servant, for she worked with the poorest people in the world in India. She served the sick and the hurting. God says that when you serve the least important among us, you are really serving him. Worship God by being a servant.

Lord, I may not totally understand all of the things that go into truly worshipping you, but I want to know, so please give me a worshipping heart. Amen.

WORSHIP ONLY ONE GOD

You shall have no other gods
before me. (Exodus 20:3, NIV)

Most people worship something even if they don't realize it. Sometimes kids worship famous people. Sometimes people worship riches. And sometimes people even worship themselves. They worship these things by making them the most important things in their lives.

If Jack doesn't want to go to church because all he wants to do is play video games, and he ignores all of his friends because he wants to watch movies two days straight, then Jack likely is worshipping entertainment. But God says that he only wants you to worship him. This doesn't mean that you can't play games or watch movies, but you shouldn't make them more important than God.

Lord, I want you to be number one in my life. No movie or game is cooler than you! Amen.

WORSHIPPING WITH OTHERS

I will give you thanks in the great assembly; among throngs of people I will praise you. (Psalm 35:18, NIV)

Worship can be a very personal thing. Many times it is just you praying and singing to God, but it shouldn't only be when you are by yourself. It is important to praise God even when you are surrounded by people. Often when a football player scores, he will raise his hands to heaven and tell God how grateful he is for helping him to play well. When a player does this, it is a way of not taking all the credit and giving the credit to God – and he wants everyone to know it. You can also praise and worship at church with other Christians. God enjoys it when several people worship him at the same time. Be sure to worship God, but not to only do it when you are by yourself.

Jesus, help me to know when and where is a good time to worship you. I love you. Amen.

WORSHIP FROM EVERYONE

*Let the rich of the earth feast and worship.
Bow before him, all who are mortal, all whose
lives will end as dust. (Psalm 22:29, NLT)*

Everyone will eventually bow down and worship God. Everyone will be judged by God when they die – it doesn't matter whether they were rich or poor. Money doesn't make any difference when it comes to having a relationship with God. Poor people can be evil; rich people can be faithful Christians – and the other way around.

The important thing to know is that if you don't have a lot of money, you shouldn't worry because you can still worship God. If you are wealthy, then don't let your money get in the way of worshipping God. At the final judgment, all that will matter is whether you accepted Jesus as your Savior and lived your life for him.

God, thank you that you accept all of us – rich and poor – into your kingdom. Please help me to not let my money or lack of money get in the way of worshipping you. Amen.

GIVE GLORY TO HIS NAME

Honor the Lord for the glory of his name. Worship the Lord in the splendor of his holiness. (Psalm 29:2, NLT)

God is so mighty and powerful that his very name deserves to be honored. In the Old Testament days, God's name was so respected that people didn't even speak it out loud.

As a Christian, you should desire to bring glory to God's name in everything that you do. One way to praise God's name is not to speak it when you are yelling in frustration or joking about something. Many people say the word "god" in everyday language, but they don't do it in a way that honors God. Show respect to God by glorifying his name and not by using it in a curse or a joke.

God, I give glory to your name because it is mighty and loving. Amen.

HOW WORSHIP AFFECTS YOU

Oh, the joys of those who trust the Lord, who have no confidence in the proud or in those who worship idols. (Psalm 40:4, NLT)

God loves it when you worship him. He gets excited to be close to you, but worshipping God helps you, too. God doesn't *need* you to worship him, but he loves it when you do. However, *you* need to worship God more than *he* needs it. The Bible says that a person who worships the Lord is happy and joyful, but the one who puts his hopes in things made by man will be destroyed.

By worshipping God, you plug yourself into the source of joy, happiness, truth, and fairness just like a lamp is plugged into the wall. When a person pulls away from God, he gets pushed further and further into the darkness and cannot see where he is going.

Heavenly Father, fill me with your light and truth. Help me to stay plugged into you. Amen.

OLD RULES

That first covenant between God and Israel had regulations for worship and a place of worship here on earth. (Hebrews 9:1, NLT)

In the Old Testament, there were a lot of rules for how God's people were supposed to worship him. There was a special tent to worship. Only certain people could go into the tent, people had to bring animal sacrifices in order to purify themselves, and there were many other rules about how the people could and couldn't approach God. But when Jesus came, everything changed. Now you can worship and praise God anywhere you want. You can praise him at church, at home with your family, quietly at school during lunch, or even right now wherever you are. Jesus died for everyone's sins so now you can go directly to God with your worship anytime you want. How cool is that?

Jesus, thank you for dying for my sins so that I can go directly to God and speak to him anytime I want. Amen.

LEARNING TO WORSHIP

Blessed are those who have learned to acclaim you, who walk in the light of your presence, O Lord. (Psalm 89:15, NIV)

The Bible says that those who learn to praise God are blessed. That means that one must learn how to worship. When children are young, they don't automatically know that they need to worship God. Even as adults, people might know that they should worship God, but they don't know how to worship him. You probably know that it is important to worship God, but you may not know how to do it. That's okay, you can learn.

Some ways you can learn are by reading the rest of this month's devotions. You can also talk to your pastor or Sunday school teacher about it. One of the best ways is to ask God to show you how to best worship him.

Lord, I know that it is important to worship you, so please show me how to best praise you. Amen.

BE GLAD

Worship the Lord with gladness. Come before him, singing with joy. (Psalm 100:2, NLT)

When you praise God, do it with gladness. The psalm writer said to come singing with joy. You might not always feel joyful. Bad things happen in life. You get grounded, or someone you love is sick, or you get a bad grade on a test. God understands when you feel sad, but when you come before God in church or on your own, the fact that he loves you and wants to be with you should make you so happy that you can't think about the sad things anymore. You feel glad and you sing for joy.

No matter how bad life gets, you always have God to turn to for help and you always have heaven to look forward to. Those are good enough reasons to smile. Bad things do happen, but you are promised a happy ending, so go to God with joy.

God, help me to praise you with happiness even when I don't feel like it. Give me joy and help me to smile. Amen.

PRAISE GOD FOR BEING JUST

I will thank the Lord because he is just;
I will sing praise to the name of the
Lord Most High. (Psalm 7:17, NLT)

Joseph wanted to join the acting club at school, but the teacher wouldn't let him. Joseph had blue eyes and the teacher only liked brown-eyed people. That isn't fair, is it?

Have you ever had someone treat you unfairly because of how you looked or something else that you could not control? It isn't fair. God deserves to be worshipped because he is just. This means that he is fair in everything that he does. He doesn't play favorites; he is fair to everyone. He loves anyone who loves him. Most people get treated unfairly, but they also are unfair to others sometimes, too. God is the only one who is fair all the time every time.

God, I can't control if someone is fair to me, but help me to be fair to other people. Amen.

PRAISE GOD FOR SAVING YOU

Save me so I can praise you publicly at Jerusalem's gates, so I can rejoice that you have rescued me. (Psalm 9:14, NLT)

When Jesus healed people from blindness, sickness, and even death, most of them went and told everyone they knew about how he had healed them. The word about Jesus spread to even more people, so big crowds came to see Jesus and hear him speak.

When God gets you out of bad situations, you should praise him to your brothers, sisters, friends, and classmates by telling them all about what he did for you. God helps you out because he loves you, but you show him how much you love him by praising him to those you know. It is a way of thanking him.

God, thank you for helping me out in tough situations. I know I can always count on you. Give me courage to share that great news with others. Amen.

PRAISE GOD BECAUSE OF HIS POWER

Rise up, O Lord, in all your power.
With music and singing we celebrate
your mighty acts. (Psalm 21:13, NLT)

God created the entire earth. He flooded the whole earth with water, but saved some people and animals on the ark. He parted the Red Sea, so his people, set free from Egypt, could cross on dry land. His Son came and healed sickness, raised the dead, walked on the water, and fed thousands of people with only a little food. Then, God gave up his Son to die for your sins. Do you know anyone else who could do that? God is so amazing that his power and strength are enough to cause us to worship him. The gods of many other religions are mean, and people worship them because they are afraid of being hurt by them. The one true God of the Bible is strong, but he is also loving. You should worship God because of his mighty strength and the mighty acts he has done for you.

God, you are stronger than anyone ever in the history of the world. You are mighty and can do anything. Amen.

PRAISE GOD FOR HIS MERCY

Praise the Lord! For he has heard my cry for mercy. (Psalm 28:6, NIV)

When was the last time you did something bad? Did you get caught or did you get away with it without anyone knowing? When you do something you shouldn't, God always knows even if no one else does. However, God deserves your worship because he is willing to forgive you and show you mercy if you ask for forgiveness. Mercy means undeserved kindness. You may not deserve it, but God always forgives you. In the same way, you shouldn't hold grudges against people when they hurt you; you should forgive them even if they don't deserve it. That's what God does. He is a merciful God who is there to help you even when you mess things up. Worship him because he is merciful to you.

Lord, thank you for showing me mercy when I mess up. Help me to show the same kind of mercy to others. Amen.

PRAISE GOD BECAUSE HE LOVES

Praise be to the Lord, for he showed his wonderful love to me. (Psalm 31:21, NIV)

Has God done something for you? Do you have clothes? Do you have food? Even if God had never done anything for you, he deserves praise. But just think about it for a minute ... what do you have? What has God given you? How has he blessed you? He has done so much for you whether you know it or not.

If you are reading this book, then you should love God because he loves you so much that he has allowed you to learn more about him and his love for you. God's love is not like human love that can change, because people do bad things. God's love will never change, so love him because he first loved you.

God, I choose to worship you because of your great love for me. Amen.

PRAISE IS AN ALL-DAY THING

My tongue will speak of your righteousness and of your praises all day long. (Psalm 35:28, NIV)

Worshipping God is not just something you do at church. David, the writer of this psalm, is described as being a man after God's own heart. David praised God at home and when he was out in the wilderness. Praising God can be an all-day thing. When you are at church, you can praise him. When you do well at school, you can tell him how grateful you are that he helped you. When you are with your friends, you can praise God by telling them the cool things that God has done for you. When you're at home, you can thank him for your parents and your siblings, the food on the table, and the roof over your head. Before you go to sleep at night, you can praise God for taking care of you. Praise is meant for all times of the day. See what happens when you make praising God an all-day thing!

Father, I will praise you when I wake up and when I go to sleep. I will praise you when I am alone and when I am with friends. I will praise you all day long. Amen.

PRAISE GOD EVEN WHEN YOU'RE SAD

Why am I discouraged? Why is my heart so sad?
I will put my hope in God! I will praise him
again – my Savior and my God! (Psalm 42:5, NLT)

You don't have to pretend everything is okay when you are sad. God knows all of the pain you go through. He understands how you feel. But just because you are down does not mean you should stop praising God. In fact, when you are feeling the worst you have ever felt it is often the best time to praise God. The next time you feel down, ask yourself why you are sad and then begin to praise God. You don't have to praise God because something bad happened; instead, praise God for who he is and how much he loves you *even though* something bad has happened. You will find that praising God does help you in all your troubles. David did. When he was discouraged and sad, he put his hope in God. You can, too.

Father, when I am sad I don't feel like praising, but please help me to praise you. I want to praise you in bad times too. Amen.

PRAISE GOD WHEN YOU'RE HAPPY

Then will I go to the altar of God, to God, my joy and my delight. I will praise you with the harp, O God, my God. (Psalm 43:4, NLT)

If you get good grades, win a game, or are just having fun with your family, take time to praise God when you are happy. Sometimes people forget to worship God when everything is going well because they are so excited about all the good things that are going on. They usually go to God only when bad times come.

But don't get in the habit of only praising and worshipping God when things get bad and you need help. In the Old Testament, when something good happened, someone often made an altar and thanked God at the altar as a reminder of what God had done. When things go well, you don't have to build anything; instead, just praise God!

Heavenly Father, I can get so excited sometimes, but I don't want to forget you in my excitement. You are the main reason for my joy. Amen.

PRAISE WITH OTHERS

For the choir director: Come, everyone! Clap your hands! Shout to God with joyful praise! (Psalm 47:1, NLT)

Choirs are groups of people that sing songs together. You might have seen one at church. People at church often sing together because God likes to hear his people worship together. In a world where there are many bad things like crime, hunger, and people who are hurting for different reasons, it is a wonderful sound to hear several people sing together.

The Bible points out that God doesn't want us to give up times of worshipping together (Hebrews 10:25). He loves it when his people come together to listen to his word, sing praises to him, pray, and learn. So even though it is important for you to have your own personal times of prayer and praise, you should not neglect joining with other Christians to do the same.

Father, I hope it blesses you when I sing and worship with other people. I hope it makes you smile to hear us all together at the same time. Amen.

PRAISE THROUGH SONG

Sing praises to God, sing praises; sing praises to our King, sing praises! (Psalm 47:6, NLT)

Jason was scared to sing in front of people, but his music teacher told him he had to, so he sang a few lines. Some of the other kids began to laugh at him, so he was very embarrassed.

Lots of people don't like to sing because they don't think they are any good at it, but God doesn't care if you are a good singer or a horrible singer. He enjoys it when you sing either way. In fact, if you are a bad singer he enjoys it even more. He knows you are praising him even though you know other people might not like your singing. You don't have to be an expert singer to worship God in song.

God, thank you for enjoying my worship even if I don't think I am the best singer. Amen.

DON'T STOP

I will praise you forever, O God, for what you have done. I will trust in your good name in the presence of your faithful people. (Psalm 52:9, NLT)

In the Olympics, there are two kinds of runners. Some runners run real fast for a short distance; others run slower, but run for a much longer distance. The runners who run those long distances show good examples of endurance. Endurance means that you can last a long time and that you keep going when others stop. When it comes to worshipping God, you should be like those long-distance runners. Don't stop. If things go badly, don't stop worshipping God. If things go very well, don't stop. If you are sad, happy, upset, or confused, don't stop. You will likely face a lot of different things in life, but through all of it, be like a long-distance runner: Don't ever stop worshipping God.

Jesus, help me to have endurance like long-distance runners. Help me to worship you no matter what! Amen.

PRAISE THROUGH OFFERINGS

I will sacrifice a voluntary offering to you; I will praise your name, O Lord, for it is good. (Psalm 54:6, NLT)

To sacrifice means to give something of yourself to praise God. In the Old Testament, people sacrificed animals, but nowadays offerings normally have to do with money. You give an offering of your own money to show your trust and dependence on God and not your earthly possessions.

Giving offerings is also a way to worship God because you are freely giving to him something you could use for yourself. You don't give offerings because you have to but because you want to. This is a way of praising God. It shows that you love him more than you love anything else.

Lord, I freely give my offerings to you to show you how much I admire and love you. Amen.

TELL GOD WHAT HE HAS DONE

*I will come and proclaim your mighty acts,
O Sovereign Lord; I will proclaim your
righteousness, yours alone. (Psalm 71:16, NIV)*

When you do well in school, it feels good to hear from your teachers and parents that you did a good job, doesn't it? If your best friend stood up for you when bullies were messing with you, then you would thank him, wouldn't you? If this is true of you, then do it for God, too. God is not a faraway person; he is with you at all times. When he does something good for you, praise him by telling him what an awesome job he did! If he helps you out of a tough situation, then praise him by thanking him. God doesn't need your praise, but he does desire it. Praise him because he cares about you and your life. Thank him for what he has done for you!

God, I know I forget to tell you sometimes, but you are an awesome God! Amen.

LET THE POOR PRAISE GOD

Do not let the oppressed retreat in disgrace; may the poor and needy praise your name. (Psalm 74:21, NIV)

The Bible tells many stories of people coming to the Lord and asking for forgiveness. Most of the people Jesus spent time with were not the rich or famous people; instead, he focused on those who knew they needed him because their lives were difficult and they wanted a Savior. No one thought much about these kinds of people. Jesus said that he "came to seek and save those who are lost" (Luke 19:10, NLT). If your life has been tough and you've felt lost, you should know that Jesus loves you. Don't let a tough life be an excuse to stop worshipping God. Instead, it should be something that drives you to worship God even more. Your life may have been tough, but trust in Jesus anyway. He came to save you.

God, my life has not been perfect, but I still want to believe in you and trust you anyhow. Amen.

PRAISE WITH ALL YOUR HEART

With all my heart I will praise you, O Lord my God. I will give glory to your name forever. (Psalm 86:12, NLT)

Kevin's favorite baseball player got caught cheating and using drugs to help him play better. Kevin was confused. This ball player said he was a Christian, but his actions didn't seem very Christianlike.

Kevin asked his dad why a Christian would act like that. His dad explained that sometimes people only allow God to work in some parts of their heart, but they block off other parts. The ones they block off usually end up hurting them in the end. His dad explained that you have to turn over your whole heart to fully allow God to work in your life. Worship God with your whole heart and do not hide any little bit from him.

God, please see my whole heart and help me not to close off any parts of my heart to you. Cleanse my heart and make it new again. Amen.

LET THE EARTH PRAISE GOD

Let the heavens be glad, and the earth rejoice!
Let the sea and everything in it shout his praise!
Let the fields and their crops burst out with joy!
Let the trees of the forest rustle with praise before
the Lord, for he is coming! (Psalm 96:11-13, NLT)

People are not the only things that worship God. God created all things, and all of his creations worship him. If you ever stop and take notice, you will see that nature praises God every day. The trees worship God as their branches brush together from the wind like hands that clap. The eagles praise God when they squawk as they fly. Dolphins praise God as they play in the water and splash around. Isn't it cool that everything worships God? You should worship God, too. The Bible says that if people don't worship him, then the rocks will! Don't let a rock do your job. Worship God, the Creator of all things!

Lord, I don't want a rock doing my job. I worship you and praise you along with all the animals and trees! Amen.

PRAISE BY OBEYING

Yes, praise the Lord, you armies of angels who serve him and do his will! (Psalm 103:21, NLT)

Maybe you want to worship God, but you don't know how. Praise and worship is not only singing and playing music. Living your life as a servant of God and obeying his will are also important ways to worship.

Just as the armies of angels praise God constantly by doing God's will, so when you obey God, you are praising him. He notices every small act of obedience, even if no one else does. He sees the little kindness you do for your sister by letting her have the last cookie. He notices the nice text message you send to encourage your friend. He sees when you help your mom without being asked. And every moment when you do those things is an act of worship. When you walk in obedience, you are worshipping God every moment of every day.

Lord, I pray for your will to be done in my life. Help me to walk in obedience and worship every day. Amen.

PRAISE BY LIVING RIGHT

The fear of the Lord is the beginning of wisdom; all who follow his precepts have good understanding. To him belongs eternal praise. (Psalm 111:10, NIV)

Having a healthy fear of the Lord is one way to worship God. This kind of fear isn't like being scared of the dark; it's more like having a lot of respect for the Lord. When you respect God, you desire to follow his precepts (which means his commands). When you live by obeying his commands of loving others, controlling your temper, being kind, and treating others like yourself, then you praise God by living right.

Lots of people can sing, but fewer people live out their worship through their actions. When you live right, you worship God and set a good example for everyone.

Lord, give me the strength to praise you by how I live my life. Amen.

PRAISE THROUGH YOUR TALENTS

Let them praise his name with dancing and make music to him with tambourine and harp. (Psalm 149:3, NIV)

Another great way to worship God is through your talents. Many times athletes, musicians, and actors use their talents only for themselves. Your talents were given to you by God, also. God loved you enough to bless you with talents, gifting, and skills. Your talents might be different than other people's, but that is okay. Worship God in all that you do, because you are able to do those things thanks to God. Just as the musicians in God's temple praised God with the talents they had for playing musical instruments, you praise God when you play sports well and honestly, when you take good care of the kids you baby-sit, when you play your instrument, when you write your poetry ... do you see? Any talent you have is from God, and you praise him when you use it in ways that honor him.

Jesus, thank you for blessing me with talents. Use the ones I have for your will and please show me other gifts that I am not even aware of. Amen.

DON'T WORSHIP IDOLS

Half of the wood he burns in the fire; over it he prepares his meal … . From the rest he makes a god, his idol; he bows down to it and worships. He prays to it and says, "Save me; you are my god." (Isaiah 44:16-17, NIV)

In the Old Testament, people made idols out of wood and worshipped them. That might sound silly to you, but people in different parts of the world still worship statues, animals, and even the sun and moon. It does not make God happy to see his people worship things that he made but forget to worship him. You might think, "I would never worship a piece of wood," but do you worship your baseball bat? That is, do you spend more time with it than you do with God? Is anything more important than God? If so, then that thing is an idol.

Only worship the one true God. All other gods are fakes. The truth from the true God can be found only in the Bible. Worship God, not idols.

Lord, I only want to worship you. It is silly to pray to a piece of wood or an animal because wood burns and animals die, but you are always here with me. Amen.

DON'T WORSHIP MAN'S IDEAS

Their worship is a farce, for they teach man-made ideas as commands from God. (Matthew 15:9, NLT)

The Bible says that not everyone who prays in Jesus' name is a Christian, because sometimes people use God to try to get things they want. Some people pretend they are helping God to get money, and sometimes they do it to get people to obey them.

This is why it is important to read the Bible yourself. Do not worship the ideas created by mankind. Only worship God. To do this, you need to learn the Bible so you can see if someone is really following God or just pretending. It is sad that people try to use God to trick people, but you can help other people by leading them to the truth of God and away from the liars.

Jesus, help me to worship your truth and not the made-up lies of bad men. Amen.

NOVEMBER

BACK TO THE FUTURE (PREPARING FOR YOUR LIFE)

WORRY

That is why I tell you not to worry about everyday life – whether you have enough food and drink, or enough clothes to wear. Isn't life more than food, and your body more than clothing? (Matthew 6:25, NLT)

Carlos was always worrying about his future. He wondered what high school would be like and he worried about what job he would get when he was older. Carlos thought about these things so much that his grades started to slip and he had problems sleeping at night because of all his worrying.

Don't worry about your future, because if you do you can't concentrate on what you are doing now. God has a plan for your life, so take it one day at a time. God doesn't want you to worry, because when you worry it shows that you aren't trusting God. He promises to guide you, watch over you, and take care of you. So relax. He has it all under control. Your job is to stay close to him.

Lord, help me to trust you and not worry about my future. Amen.

DISCOVERING GOD'S PLAN

Trust in the Lord with all your heart; do not depend on your own understanding. Seek his will in all you do, and he will show you which path to take. (Proverbs 3:5-6, NLT)

You might be wondering about what the future holds and what you will be when you grow up. You might be saying, "How will I know what God wants for me?" Don't worry. God is not going to try to keep a secret from you and play games. He *wants* you to follow his will and he promises to guide you. All you should focus on is doing what the Bible tells you to do now.

Honor your parents, work hard, and obey God. Then let God show you his will by opening the doors you are supposed to walk through. God has an amazing plan for you, but he almost never tells you every part of his plan all at once. He wants you to trust him step by step.

Jesus, I don't need to know every detail, but please show me what the next step for me is. Help me to hear you correctly and to follow you. Amen.

WORKING HARD

Work willingly at whatever you do, as though you were working for the Lord rather than for people. (Colossians 3:23, NLT)

Most of the people in the Bible had no idea what they would end up doing. Moses and David were shepherds, Gideon was in the family business, and Peter was a fisherman. All of these men became great men of God – leaders, kings, judges, missionaries. One thing they all have in common is that at one time they had normal everyday jobs. They weren't superstars. They were just regular guys. This shows that God uses people who work hard at whatever they're doing. These guys weren't lazy. Being a shepherd or a fisherman was hard work. God then called them to other tasks. When you don't know what you should do, then work hard at what you're doing right now. If you are doing chores or working at school, work as if you were working for the Lord.

God, help me to be a hard worker. Show me what that really means. Use me, because I want to do your will. Amen.

DEALING WITH THE UNKNOWN

So don't worry about tomorrow, for tomorrow will bring its own worries. Today's trouble is enough for today. (Matthew 6:34, NLT)

Jeff was always worrying about tomorrow. He worried about school and about tests. He worried about getting his homework done. He worried if his friends and teachers liked him. He just always worried. And you know what? When "tomorrow" came, it was "today," and Jeff decided to keep on worrying – about tomorrow!

That's a silly way to live. Don't worry about tomorrow. Jesus said that when you get to tomorrow, you can deal with it then and there, because then it will be "today." And most of the time, the things you worry about don't happen anyway, so you just wasted a whole lot of time worrying. Instead, trust God with tomorrow. And then, trust him with today.

God, I know I shouldn't worry about tomorrow, but please be patient with me and help me to get over my fear. Help me today, and help me trust you for tomorrow. Amen.

DEALING WITH MISTAKES

We all stumble in many ways. If anyone is never at fault in what he says, he is a perfect man, able to keep his whole body in check. (James 3:2, NIV)

Whenever Manny walked down the stairs, he always held on tightly to the handrail to help keep him from falling. Manny had a fear of missing a step, and every now and then he would, but his grip on the handrail kept him from stumbling down the stairs. As you get older, you will make mistakes. You will "stumble in many ways," as the Bible says. In fact, that's pretty normal, because no one is perfect. Some people are so afraid of messing up that it controls their life. Don't be like that; don't let fear control you. You aren't perfect, so don't put that pressure on yourself. But if you hold on to God, he will help protect you from falling too far, just like Manny's handrail.

Jesus, I want to do the right thing so much that I worry about messing up. Please help me not to get so down about mistakes. Help me to hold on to you. Amen.

GIVING GOD YOUR DREAM

Delight yourself in the Lord and he will give you the desires of your heart. Commit your way to the Lord; trust in him and he will do this. (Psalm 37:4-5, NIV)

Do you already know what you want to be when you grow up? What is it? A doctor, actor, athlete, pastor, or something else? If you already think you know what you want to be, then give it over to God. Sometimes guys make their dream into their god (which then makes it an idol in their lives), and they will do anything to make that dream happen. However, if you give your dream to God, then you allow him to make your path known. You allow him to either adjust your dream toward his will, or to prepare the path toward what you desire. It's better to have God on your side instead of trying to do everything on your own. There is nothing wrong with having big dreams, but make sure your heart is right first.

Father, I give all of my hopes and dreams over to you. Amen.

HANDLING DISAPPOINTMENTS

*Never will I leave you; never will
I forsake you. (Hebrews 13:5, NIV)*

Jake was really sad because his grandma died a week before his birthday party. He loved his grandma very much, and he cried when he heard the bad news. Jake didn't understand why people had to die.

Life is not a fairy tale. Sometimes you get disappointed because bad things happen. And death is a part of life – everyone faces it at some time. Jake knew that his grandma was a Christian and that made him happy because he knew that she was with Jesus in heaven. He still missed her a lot, and he still cried once in a while. Death is a very sad thing, but God was with his grandma, and God was with Jake, too. No matter what happens, God will always be with you. Even in your hardest, saddest moment in life, God is with you. All you have to do is call out to him.

God, hear my prayers and see my tears. I don't understand a lot of things, but let me always be able to call to you when I am sad. Amen.

HAPPY THROUGH DISCIPLINE

Blessed is the man you discipline, O Lord, the man you teach from your law. (Psalm 94:12, NIV)

Frank was having a bad week. His teachers were giving so much homework and his dad kept piling chores on him. Frank got really mad and lost his temper. He yelled at his mom, and then he got grounded! As Frank sat in his room, he realized that not only was his mom disciplining him for yelling at her, but God was disciplining him too – for his bad attitude. He knew he needed to change his thinking. He understood that God gave him the opportunity to learn at school and that he had great parents who just wanted to help him. He thanked God for disciplining him and showing him how to live better.

The Bible says that a man God disciplines is blessed, for it shows how much God loves him. When you make mistakes and God disciplines you, ask him to help you to grow from it.

Lord, when you have to discipline me, show me what I need to learn from the experience so that I can be a better person. Amen.

SAYING GOOD-BYE

So they said good-bye to Rebekah and sent her away with Abraham's servant and his men. The woman who had been Rebekah's childhood nurse went along with her. (Genesis 24:59, NLT)

Brett was excited to start middle school because he liked to think he was now mature and grown up. He also wanted to see all of his friends. But then, during the summer, he learned that all but one of his friends was moving away. He had to say good-bye to them, and Brett felt sad and empty. He loved the memories he had of great times with those guys.

As you grow up, you will have to say many good-byes. Life changes a lot, so enjoy the time you have with your friends today. Good-byes may come, but you fill in the empty feeling with memories of good times. Then move on. God has other friends for you to meet and other memories for you to make.

God, I know you are in control of my life, so please help me to be able to say good-bye when I need to. Amen.

STAYING GROUNDED

When [Peter] realized [the angel had freed him from prison], he went to the home of Mary, the mother of John Mark, where many were gathered for prayer. (Acts 12:12, NLT)

You need to have roots, like a big tree, because when life gets tough, you don't want to get pushed over. You grow roots by getting closer to God, but also by being actively involved in a church and surrounding yourself with Christian friends.

When the early church was being persecuted and Peter had been thrown in prison, the believers got together and prayed. When Peter was miraculously freed, he knew right where to find his friends – they were together praying for him. When times get tough, your friends and your church are ways God uses to get you past the hard times. Put down your roots. They will keep you grounded.

Lord, help me to have roots that will keep me grounded through tough times. Amen.

LOVING YOUR PARENTS

Anyone who steals from his father and mother and says, "What's wrong with that?" is no better than a murderer. (Proverbs 28:24, NLT)

God thinks so highly of parents that he chose to reveal himself as one. God the Father is the main way he shows himself to you.

In the Bible, he says that children should honor their parents and treat them right. He even says that if you obey your parents, you'll have a longer life. But God wants you to go further than just obeying your parents; he wants you to love them, too. Love them when they mess up and make mistakes. Love them even if they are no longer around. And above all, don't justify doing things against them – like stealing money from your mom's purse – because you are trying to get back at them for something. Your parents may not be perfect (no parents are), but God has put them in your life for a reason. Honor God by honoring your parents.

Jesus, help me to love my parents even when it is hard. Amen.

BEING HEALTHY

*You must serve only the Lord your God. If you do,
I will bless you with food and water, and I will
protect you from illness. (Exodus 23:25, NLT)*

Kevin needed to mow the lawn, but he also needed to get fuel for the lawnmower. He first put sand in the mower, but it didn't work. Then he tried to put mud in it, and still it wouldn't go. Finally, Kevin put jelly in the mower, and it didn't work then either. It's pretty silly to think that all he needed to do was put gas in the mower. The mower was made to use a certain kind of fuel in order to run well.

The same is true of your body. It needs good fuel, too. God made your body to work a certain way, so you shouldn't eat too much junk because it's not healthy for you. Try to eat less fried and junk foods and more fruits and vegetables. See how much better you feel!

Lord, show me how to make better choices in what I eat so my body will work the way you created it to. Amen.

THE SEASONS OF LIFE

There is a time for everything, and a season for every activity under heaven. (Ecclesiastes 3:1, NIV)

Jack and his family moved to Indiana. It was very different for him, because he had lived in Florida for most of his life. It was new for him to experience four distinct seasons. He was used to it being warm all the time. In Indiana, it was warm for spring and summer, but in the fall it got cool, and the leaves on the trees turned to different colors. Winter was very cold and snowy. Every season was very different and beautiful in its own way.

The Bible says that there will be different seasons in your life, too. Sometimes it will be nice and everything seems great. At other times, it might be cold and lonely. God made all of the seasons, so see what he is teaching you in every season of your life. Each one is beautiful in its own way because God is with you. He has a reason for the season.

Lord, help me to see what you are teaching me in this season of life right now. Amen.

GIVING TO GIVE

Some people are always greedy for more, but the godly love to give! (Proverbs 21:26; NLT)

Sam gave Jacob some of his pizza because he was hoping Jacob would give him some of his nachos, but that didn't happen. Jacob took the pizza, but gave the rest of his nachos to a girl who sat behind them. Sam was angry. He had only given Jacob his pizza so he could get some nachos. It's a difficult lesson to learn: Don't give to get.

Don't give someone something if you are just trying to get something else. When you give, give with no expectation that you will get anything in return. God gives you stuff because he wants to bless you, so give to others because you want to bless them.

Jesus, help me to give just to give and not to get back, because I don't want to be selfish to others. Amen.

OFFER YOUR TALENTS TO GOD

God works in different ways, but it is the same God who does the work in all of us. A spiritual gift is given to each of us so we can help each other. (1 Corinthians 12:6-7, NLT)

There were two guys who were great musicians. One decided to be a missionary in Asia and used his music to tell kids about Jesus. The other musician became a huge star and made lots of money.

Who was the bigger success? The star made lots of money, but he never honored God. He never helped anybody, but instead spent all his money on himself. The missionary didn't make a lot of money or play to huge crowds, but he helped lots of kids learn about Jesus. True success is what God sees as success. If you give your talents and skills to God, he will use them. God's plans for your talents may be different than yours, but his plan is true success.

Lord, help me to give you my talents. Whatever you want me to do, please help me to desire your will. Amen.

HAVING FAITH

*Everything is possible for him
who believes. (Mark 9:23, NIV)*

The king needed a brave man to rescue his daughter, the princess. He summoned two knights, Marcus and William, telling them that there was a bridge near the canyon that they had to cross in order to save the princess. Marcus was good looking and very athletic, but William was not.

When they got to the canyon, they couldn't see a bridge. Marcus turned back, but William had faith that if the king said there was a bridge, there must be a bridge. William stepped off the ledge and landed on a bridge that was almost invisible – covered with branches and moss. William crossed the bridge and saved the princess.

God can use you more if you have faith rather than just talent. If you have faith, you are willing to obey his voice.

Jesus, help me to be a man of faith who trusts in your words. Amen.

BEING KIND

Don't forget to show hospitality to strangers, for some who have done this have entertained angels without realizing it! (Hebrews 13:2, NLT)

A young man went to the castle because he wanted to speak to the king. At the door was a servant who told the young man that the castle was closed. The young man yelled at the servant, because he felt he should be able to speak to the king. Then, the servant revealed that he *was* the king! Since the young man had been mean to a servant, the king refused to speak to him as well.

God wants you to be kind to everyone regardless of who they are, because they are God's creations and deserve to be treated with respect. Even more, the Bible says that sometimes you might even entertain an angel without realizing it!

Jesus, help me to be kind to others because they are your creations. Besides, I never know when I might actually be talking to an angel! Amen.

MISSION - NOT IMPOSSIBLE

And then [Jesus] told them, "Go into all the world and preach the Good News to everyone." (Mark 16:15, NLT)

Jesus told his disciples that they should tell everyone about him. He didn't want the Good News just to be told to those close by, but to all parts of the world. If you don't know what you want to be when you grow up, you should pray about going on a missions trip. This allows you to tell people about Jesus, but God might just reveal to you what he has planned for your life.

When you are actively involved in doing God's work, then he has a way of showing you new things you haven't seen yet. Talk to your parents about opportunities that come up at church for a family mission trip, or a trip you could save for when you get a little older. Ask God to show you what he would like you to do.

God, if you want me to go on a missions trip, please help me know what to do and where to go. Amen.

USING TIME WISELY

For we are each responsible for our own conduct. (Galatians 6:5, NLT)

Three friends had a test the next day, but while one was studying very hard, the other two friends spent the night playing video games. The next morning, the boy who studied got a good grade, but the other two failed the test.

You are getting older now, so it's time you started to get a little more responsible. You must learn to use your time wisely. Time is one thing that you can't get back – because once a second passes, it's gone forever. Sit down and talk to your parents about how you can best use your time wisely.

Lord, show me how to use my time wisely. Amen.

TREAT ELDERS WELL

Stand up in the presence of the elderly, and show respect for the aged. Fear your God. I am the Lord. (Leviticus 19:32, NLT)

Drake was at a party for his dad's work and he was telling everyone what a great baseball player he was. An older man was very interested, asked Drake some questions and tried to give him some advice. But Drake ignored him and kept talking about himself. He didn't think an old guy could teach him anything about baseball. Later that evening, Drake's dad told him that the old guy was a hall of fame baseball hitter. Drake realized he could have learned some tips from that old pro. Some young people don't understand that older people have a lot to offer; they have experienced so much in life and have learned a lot of hard lessons. God says that older people deserve your respect. Show respect by listening to older people, asking questions, and learning from what they have learned.

Lord, I want to respect the older people I know. Help me to learn as much as I can from them. Amen.

UNPLUGGING DISTRACTIONS

Only in returning to me and resting in me will you be saved. In quietness and confidence is your strength. (Isaiah 30:15, NLT)

With all of the iPods, video games, TV, movies, and other distractions, a kid could go the whole day and not talk to anyone. Many times, kids can't help but talk to parents and teachers, but they get so wrapped up in electronics that they forget to talk to God.

In the Old Testament, when God wanted to get his people's attention, he told them to return to him and rest in him. In quietness and confidence they would find strength, for in the quietness, they could focus on him. During this next week, unplug from all of the electronics and anything else that distracts from your prayer time. Make a special effort to read your Bible and talk to God. After a week is over, schedule a time that you will spend with God every day. Unplug from everything else and plug into God!

Lord, help me to unplug and focus on you. I don't want anything to be more important than you. Amen.

PRAY ABOUT THE FUTURE

*"For I know the plans I have for you," says the Lord.
"They are plans for good and not for disaster, to give
you a future and a hope." (Jeremiah 29:11, NLT)*

You can plan all you want about the future, but until it happens, you really don't know what it looks like. Since you don't know what will happen, you should pray for your future. Pray that God will direct you and that you won't be afraid. God listens to prayer, and praying for your future is important.

God promises that he already knows the plans he has for you. Don't be afraid of God's plans. He isn't out to get you or to make you miserable. His plans are for good and not disaster, they are to give you a future and a hope. Pray that God will walk with you step by step and show you which paths to take. He knows the plan. He will get you to your destination.

Jesus, guide my steps and bless them even before I take them. Amen.

VOLUNTEERING

I assisted the poor in their need and the orphans who required help. (Job 29:12, NLT)

You might not have a lot of money to give, but one of the greatest offerings you can give to God is your time. Your time is valuable, so God appreciates it when you donate your time to tasks that honor him.

God wants his people to help those in need. Donate your time to help out at a shelter or in your church. Volunteering helps you to give to other people. This is important because many young people only think about themselves. When you volunteer to help those in need, you are thinking about the needs of others. Jesus said that when you help others, it's like you are helping him. That is a great privilege. Talk to your parents about where you might be able to volunteer and serve those less fortunate.

Lord, give me a heart to volunteer to help others, and then show me where I can be of help. Amen.

HAVING DISCERNMENT

Test everything. Hold on to the good. Avoid every kind of evil. (1 Thessalonians 5:21-22, NIV)

Timothy liked to watch movies, but he wasn't smart about which movies to watch and which movies not to watch. He watched everything. However, one night he watched a scary movie that he couldn't forget, so for the next week he had trouble sleeping because he was so afraid.

You need to have discernment, which means being wise and careful. You think about whether something is good for you or not. If it is, then you hold onto it; if it isn't, then you avoid or get rid of it. You need to be careful about what kinds of things you allow yourself to watch. Your parents might help you with that, but they aren't always around, so you must learn to make good choices on your own. If there's anything that you don't think God would like, then don't watch it. It's better to be safe than sorry.

Lord, guard my eyes so I don't see anything I shouldn't. Help me to make good decisions about what I watch. Amen.

BEING THANKFUL

Be thankful in all circumstances, for this is God's will for you who belong to Christ Jesus. (1 Thessalonians 5:18, NLT)

One day, Mrs. Green made a batch of cookies for Sean. He was so thankful that she made him another batch the next day. She was so impressed with his gratitude that she made him other foods, too.

God likes to give good gifts to you, and he likes it even more when you remember to be thankful. When you are truly thankful, God wants to bless you again. Take the time today to thank God for everything you have. Don't worry about what you don't have. Just focus on all the things God has blessed you with. Show you are thankful by telling him.

God, thank you so much for everything you have given me. Thanks for my family, food, home, and Jesus! Amen.

DON'T RUSH

A prudent man gives thought to his steps. (Proverbs 14:15, NIV)

Pen was a kangaroo who liked to make quick decisions and jump into things before he fully understood them. One day, Pen didn't see where he was going and he jumped right into an animal trap. Pen didn't take time to see where he was going, so he got caught.

You might want to make things happen *now*, and so you try to do things to make them hurry up and happen right away. The problem is that you are rushing ahead of God's timing. He will do the right things for you in the right way at just the right time. The Bible says that smart people give a lot of thought to their steps. That means they pray about it, think about it, and get advice before they make a decision.

God, keep me from rushing things. Let me trust your timing on everything. Amen.

FINISHING STRONG

I have fought the good fight, I have finished the race, I have kept the faith. (2 Timothy 4:7, NIV)

A king told his workers that there would be a special feast for a special guest, so when work was over with, they would all celebrate. Most of the workers were excited, so they left work early to go to the party, but Nicholas stayed until his job was finished. When the king announced the special guest, they were surprised to see Nicholas! The king wanted to honor him for his hard work and for staying on his job until it was finished.

You honor God when you finish the work that you've started. When the apostle Paul wrote his very last letter, he told Timothy confidently that he had fought the good fight, finished the race, and kept the faith. God is honored when you persevere from now all through your life.

Father, I don't want to be a quitter. I want to persevere with you all the days of my life. Amen.

TEAMWORK

For we are God's fellow workers; you are God's field, God's building. (1 Corinthians 3:9, NIV)

One guy tried to carry a heavy box, but he couldn't by himself. Then another guy came to help him. They could move it, but it was tough. Then a third guy came to help, and the three men were able to carry the box fairly easily. Teamwork helps you get more done. God believes in teamwork. After all, he didn't pick one disciple, he picked twelve. And when he first sent his followers out to share the Good News, he sent them in pairs, not by themselves. In 1 Corinthians, Paul writes about how some people plant a seed (tell others about Jesus), others help it grow (act as good friends, be consistent in their faith as an example), and still others bring in the harvest (pray with the person to become a Christian). But the important thing is that people are saved because each person willingly does his part. Through it you're doing God's work and he is honored.

Lord, help me to be a team player. I will do the tasks you assign for me – and I will do them well! Amen.

BEING SMART ON THE INTERNET

Don't be misled – you cannot mock the justice of God. You will always harvest what you plant. Those who live only to satisfy their own sinful nature will harvest decay and death from that sinful nature. But those who live to please the Spirit will harvest everlasting life from the Spirit. (Galatians 6:7-8, NLT)

Ken liked to talk to his friends on the Internet. One day, Ken got upset at one of his friends, so he posted a lot of mean things. Then some people started sticking up for his friend and saying bad things about Ken. Ken got mad and said more bad things until pretty soon everyone was mad!

The Bible says that you will harvest what you plant. Ken planted anger and malice, and that's what he got in return. When you use the Internet, be careful what you post for others to see. It's best to talk with your parents to find out what is okay and what is not. You should be an example of Jesus on the Internet just like you should in real life.

Father, please help me to use the Internet wisely. Amen.

JUST SAY NO

Stay away from a foolish man, for you will not find knowledge on his lips. (Proverbs 14:7, NIV)

Craig's friends wanted him to start smoking, but he said no. He saw how much it hurt the adults he knew who were addicted to smoking. Many of those adults wanted to stop, but they couldn't. Addiction means that, even though a person wants to stop doing something, he can't because his body has gotten used to it and thinks it needs it. When he tries to stop, he gets very sick, so he goes back to whatever he is addicted to in order to feel better. Alcohol, smoking, and drugs are just some examples of things people get addicted to. When someone asks you to do something you know is wrong, just say no. God doesn't want you to become a slave to these things. God wants you to be free. Learn the great power of the little word "no."

Jesus, keep me far away from things that can cause addiction, but help me to say no if someone does offer them to me. Amen.

DECEMBER

FOLLOW THE LEADER
(JESUS' EXAMPLE)

CALLED BEFORE BIRTH

She will give birth to a son, and you are to give him the name Jesus, because he will save his people from their sins. (Matthew 1:21, NIV)

God sent his angels to tell Mary and Joseph about the plan he had for saving people from sin. God knew what the plan was, because he is all-knowing. Before Jesus was even born, God had thought out who his parents were going to be, where he would live, and even what his parents should name him! God had a plan for Jesus, and he has a plan for you, too.

In the Old Testament, God told Jeremiah that he had plans for him even before he was born (Jeremiah 1:4), so God has a pattern of having plans for his children. Don't worry about what the plan is, but rather work on being willing to follow it once you do know. You can start today by obeying God in whatever task he has for you.

Lord, prepare my heart for the plans you have for my life. Make me aware of them when the time comes. Amen.

JESUS WAS HUMBLE

Jesus came from Galilee to the Jordan to be baptized by John. (Matthew 3:13, NIV)

Jesus is the Son of God. He healed the sick, raised people from the dead, died for sinners, and made a huge impact on the history of the world. But Jesus was also humble. He did not walk around acting like he was super important.

Jesus actually allowed himself to be baptized by John the Baptist. John even felt unworthy to baptize Jesus, but Jesus wanted to do things the right way, so he humbled himself in order to be an example to his followers.

You should take note about how Jesus handled himself. Be humble even when you are good at things. Show respect to other people even if you are better than them in sports or in school. Jesus is your example.

Lord, help me to be more like you. Give me a humble spirit in everything that I do. Amen.

JESUS DIDN'T CUT CORNERS

Jesus replied, "Let it be so now; it is proper for us to do this to fulfill all righteousness." Then John consented. (Matthew 3:15, NIV)

When John the Baptist didn't want to baptize Jesus, Jesus convinced him that it was the right thing to do. Jesus didn't cut corners. He didn't cheat. He didn't do anything half way. When Jesus was baptized, God the Father said that he was pleased with Jesus. Shortly after that, Jesus started his public ministry. You might grow up to be a pastor, athlete, actor, teacher, or a scientist, but no matter what you end up doing, make sure that you do things the right way. Do what you know is right. Don't cut corners. Don't take the short path if that means doing something wrong or avoiding something you know you should do.

Jesus, I know you didn't cut corners. Please give me the strength to always do the right thing, even if it might be embarrassing or difficult. Amen.

JESUS PLEASED HIS FATHER

A voice from heaven said, "This is my Son, whom I love; with him I am well pleased." (Matthew 3:17, NIV)

God was pleased with his Son Jesus, and he let everyone know about it. Jesus was a good Son. He obeyed, he learned Scripture, he took care of his mother, and he gave God the respect he deserved.

Some kids have a close relationship with their dads and some do not, but either way you can have a great relationship with your heavenly Father. If you want to please God, then look at Jesus for a good example of how to be a good son.

Don't be concerned with trying to be perfect, because God knows that you will make mistakes sometimes, but never lose your desire to please your heavenly Father.

Heavenly Father, I want to please you in all that I do. I pray for strength to be more and more like Christ so that I please you in my words and actions. Amen.

JESUS FACED TEMPTATION

Jesus was led by the Spirit into the desert to be tempted by the devil. (Matthew 4:1, NIV)

When you are with your friends, or even when you are alone, you may be tempted to do something you know is wrong. Adam and Eve were tempted. Temptation is a part of living in a sinful world. However, you don't have to give in to your temptations. Being tempted is not a sin; after all,

Jesus was tempted and he never sinned. He was led out into the wilderness and the devil tried to make all sorts of deals with him to get Jesus to turn to his side, but Jesus resisted. Because Jesus resisted, you can resist doing bad things, too. When you are tempted, ask God to help you overcome the pressures that you feel.

Jesus, give me your strength to keep from sinning. I don't want to cheat, be jealous, or do anything that would displease you. Amen.

JESUS UNDERSTOOD THE BIBLE

Jesus responded, "The Scriptures also say, 'You must not test the Lord your God.'" (Matthew 4:7, NLT)

When Jesus was being tested by the devil, the devil offered him riches and power, but Jesus turned him down. The devil even tried to use Scripture to trick Jesus, but that didn't work either. Jesus battled the devil with the ultimate sword, the sword of truth – the Bible. Jesus knew God's word, so he knew when the devil was using God's word the wrong way. Then Jesus used it the right way in order to fight off Satan's lies and temptations.

Scripture is the best weapon you can use when you are in trouble. If you are being tempted to sin, the Bible gives you the words to fight off those attacks by telling you what is right to do. Jesus had the strongest weapon of all – God's word – and so do you. The more you know it, the better prepared you will be.

God, show me how to use the Bible. It is such a big book; please teach me how to use it. Amen.

JESUS SPOKE THE TRUTH

From then on Jesus began to preach, "Repent of your sins and turn to God, for the Kingdom of Heaven is near." (Matthew 4:17, NLT)

Politicians on TV often say anything to get people to vote for them, even if what they say isn't true. They do this so people will like them and vote for them.

Jesus was not a politician. He didn't try to get people to like him. He told them the truth. He spoke a lot about turning away from sin and turning to God.

Some people don't like to be told that they are doing something wrong, and lots of people didn't like Jesus for that reason. You don't have to be annoying to people, but when you have an opportunity to tell the truth, you shouldn't hesitate. If you speak the truth people might not like it, but you are doing what Jesus did.

Jesus, help me to be honest and speak your truth, but to do so in love. I don't want to be mean, so show me how to do that. Amen.

JESUS SAW PEOPLE'S POTENTIAL

Jesus called out to them, "Come, follow me, and I will show you how to fish for people!" (Matthew 4:19, NLT)

When you see a homeless person, do you ever wonder what his talents are? Back in Jesus' day, these fishermen were hard workers, but no one wanted their autographs. However, when Jesus saw them, he didn't just see men who fished for a living, he saw what they could become.

Jesus sees the potential in people. He sees the good things he wants to do with your life. He sees the talents he gave you and has plans for how he wants you to use them for his glory. He also wants you to see the potential in other people, too. Look at your friends as Jesus does – see them with lots of potential. Encourage them to be all that God wants them to be.

God, thank you for seeing my potential. Give me your eyes to help me see people like you see them. Amen.

JESUS HEALED

Jesus went throughout Galilee, teaching in their synagogues, preaching the good news of the kingdom, and healing every disease and sickness among the people. (Matthew 4:23, NIV)

In the movies, Wolverine could heal himself when he got hurt, but he couldn't heal other people. Jesus had the power to heal people and even bring them back from the dead. Unlike Wolverine, who is a fictional character, Jesus is real. Jesus healed the blind and those who couldn't walk. He healed people who had a skin disease. He cast out demons. He helped people who couldn't hear or speak. He healed so many people that the Bible doesn't even record all of them. Jesus can heal you, too. He can heal any hurts that you have from mean words said by friends or family members. He can heal any disappointments you might have from people you care about. If you are lonely he can heal that, too. All you need to do is ask him.

Jesus, I need you to heal me. Please touch my heart and fix my pain. Amen.

JESUS SPENT TIME WITH FAMILY

When he saw the crowds, he went up on a mountainside and sat down. His disciples came to him. (Matthew 5:1, NLT)

You are starting to grow up. You probably have friends who want you to hang out with them and, as you continue to get older, that will happen more and more.

Jesus had lots of people who wanted to spend time with him, but he knew it was important to spend time with those who he was closest to. It is okay to want to goof off with friends, but don't forget to spend quality time with your family and your closest Christian friends. Families and good friends help you to grow to be a strong Christian young man. God wants you to have friends, but remember to spend quality time with those closest to you.

God, thank you for my friends and family. Bless the time I spend with them and help us to have fun. Amen.

JESUS WAS NOT IN A CLIQUE

When he came down from the mountainside, large crowds followed him. (Matthew 8:1, NIV)

Jesus had close friends, but he wasn't into cliques. A clique is when you and a few friends only hang out with each other and do not act kindly to those not in your special group. Jesus spent quality time with his closest friends, but he spent a lot of time with other people, too.

It's okay to have good friends, but sometimes it is also important to spend time with people outside of your special group of friends. You should so that you won't get pegged as part of a clique. You can reach out to that one kid who always sits alone at lunch or someone else who seems to need friends. Jesus did that, so follow his example.

Jesus, I don't want to be selfish in my relationships. If there is someone who could use me as a friend, then please show me who that is. Amen.

JESUS HELPED SICK PEOPLE

A man with leprosy approached him. "Lord," the man said, "if you are willing, you can heal me and make me clean." Jesus reached out and touched him. "I am willing," he said. "Be healed!". (Matthew 8:2-3, NLT)

Leprosy was one of the most feared diseases in the Bible times because it could spread from one person to another through touch. Because it was so contagious and dangerous, people with leprosy had to leave their families and live in a place with other lepers. This man who came to Jesus didn't even know if Jesus would come near him. Jesus actually touched and healed him.

Sometimes if you go to a hospital or visit a retirement home for elderly people, it can be kind of scary. But if you try to be like Jesus, then you shouldn't be afraid of sick people. Sick people are just like you, but they are ill and need help. The most important thing is that they need your love. Try to love like Jesus did.

God, I want to love those who are sick, because you love them, too. Amen.

JESUS COMPLIMENTED OTHERS

When Jesus heard this, he was astonished and said to those following him, "I tell you the truth, I have not found anyone in Israel with such great faith." (Matthew 8:10, NIV)

You know that Jesus is the Son of God and that he died for your sins, but some people didn't even believe Jesus when he was on earth. When Jesus saw that someone had faith, he complimented the person. In this case, he was complimenting a Roman soldier who trusted that Jesus could heal his servant by just speaking a word. Jesus was amazed – that was stronger faith than he had found among the people of Israel, who should have believed in him. You are like Jesus when you give sincere compliments to people.

Many people don't like to say good things about other people because they feel bad about themselves, but Jesus was not afraid to encourage those who impressed him.

Jesus, help me to encourage people when they do well. Show me how to give sincere compliments. Amen.

JESUS CARED FOR HIS ELDERS

When Jesus arrived at Peter's house, Peter's mother-in-law was sick in bed with a high fever. But when Jesus touched her hand, the fever left her. Then she got up and prepared a meal for him. (Matthew 8:14-15, NLT)

Jesus healed kids, soldiers, and even those who were older than him. Peter's mother-in-law was sick, so Jesus took the time to heal her fever. Jesus didn't have to do that. After all, a fever is not nearly as big of a deal as raising the dead or healing the blind. She might have just gotten better on her own after a little while. But Jesus honored those older than himself. Jesus was the Messiah, but he still showed respect to his elders.

When you're young, it is easy to think that you have all the answers. You aren't the only one who doesn't like to be told what to do all the time, but God wants you to respect your elders.

Lord, I want to honor you by honoring my elders. Please help me to keep a good attitude toward those older than me. Amen.

JESUS SCARED THE BAD GUYS

That evening many demon-possessed people were brought to Jesus. He cast out the evil spirits with a simple command. (Matthew 8:16, NLT)

What scares you? When you were younger, maybe you were scared of the dark. Now maybe you're scared of Tank, the big bully at school. No matter what you're scared of, it is important to remember that Jesus is on your side. Guess what? The meanest bad guys are scared of Jesus.

You can't get any worse than demons, and when Jesus just said a word to them, they had to flee. So remember, no matter how scared you get, don't forget that Jesus is stronger than the dark or any bully. God doesn't want you to live in fear; he wants you to understand that he is looking out for you.

God, I know you're more powerful than anything, so help me to just relax and trust you. Amen.

JESUS DIDN'T LIVE IN FEAR

Without warning, a furious storm came up on the lake, so that the waves swept over the boat. But Jesus was sleeping. (Matthew 8:24, NIV)

What if you were with Jesus in a boat in the middle of a huge storm with waves crashing over the deck? You'd probably be scared, right? The disciples were fishermen and were used to sailing their boat in storms, but this one was so bad that even they were scared. What was Jesus doing? He was sleeping. He wasn't afraid of the storm.

People are afraid of all sorts of things. Some people fear spiders or snakes. Others really don't like heights or small spaces. Then there are those who fear just about everything. You don't want to be afraid of everything because it prevents you from really trusting God. Jesus was not afraid of the storm. The disciples shouldn't have been afraid either, because Jesus was with them. Jesus is with you, too, so don't live in fear.

Father, I give all my fears to you. Amen!

JESUS FORGAVE SINS

Some people brought to him a paralyzed man on a mat. Seeing their faith, Jesus said to the paralyzed man, "Be encouraged, my child! Your sins are forgiven." (Matthew 9:2, NLT)

Jesus didn't just heal people; he also forgave their sins. You might think healing the paralyzed man's legs would be the first thing Jesus would do; instead, Jesus' first priority was to make sure the man's sins were forgiven. That's way more important. Jesus erased every bad thing the paralyzed man had ever done. The man was able to start all over again. Only then did Jesus also heal him so he could walk.

Jesus has forgiven your sins as well. Sin would keep you and everyone else out of heaven, but Jesus died to offer you that forgiveness. Jesus sits on the right hand of the Father and, when you go to heaven, Jesus will be on your side. After all, in order for you to be forgiven, he gave his life.

Jesus, I ask you to forgive my sins and I accept you as King of my life. You are the Son of God and you died and rose again to forgive my sins. Thank you. Amen.

JESUS KNEW PEOPLE'S THOUGHTS

Jesus knew what they were thinking, so he asked them, "Why do you have such evil thoughts in your hearts?" (Matthew 9:4, NLT)

When Jesus was ministering to people, some of the religious leaders were upset with him and started thinking evil thoughts about him. But Jesus knew what they were thinking! He asked them why they thought such evil things. You might not get in trouble at school or even at home, but maybe you allow yourself to think things that you shouldn't.

God knows what you think and, if you allow yourself to be controlled by bad thoughts, then you are still not doing the right thing. Ask God to forgive you of those bad thoughts right now, because he already knows what you have been thinking. Ask him to help you think about good things.

God, please forgive me for thinking about things that I shouldn't think about. Amen.

JESUS WASN'T POPULAR

As Jesus went on from there, he saw a man named Matthew sitting at the tax collector's booth. "Follow me," he told him, and Matthew got up and followed him. (Matthew 9:9, NIV)

Jesus asked Matthew to become one of his disciples. This might not seem like a big deal, but Matthew was a tax collector. Tax collectors were not liked at all back in the Bible times. They were often seen as traitors because they worked for the Roman government and collected taxes from their Jewish countrymen. On top of that, many of them were unfair and collected extra money that they kept for themselves. But Jesus saw into Matthew's heart. He didn't care if people liked his choice; Jesus was not trying to win a popularity contest. Jesus didn't do things that looked good; he did what God wanted him to do. Don't try to be popular. Instead, live right by following Jesus.

God, I really want people to like me, but I want you to be proud of me more, so help me to make you proud. Amen.

JESUS LOVED KIDS

*Jesus called the children to him and said,
"Let the little children come to me, and do not
hinder them, for the kingdom of God belongs
to such as these." (Luke 18:16, NIV)*

Kevin dreaded Sunday afternoon lunch with his family, because his entire family would come over to his house. This meant that he would have to eat at the kiddy table with all of the little children. Kevin felt as though no one respected him because none of the adults took the time to talk to him. When you are younger, it might feel sometimes that you are on the outside, but you should know Jesus is on your side. He didn't spend all of his time with the adults. He wanted to be with the children. The disciples tried to shoo the children away, but Jesus said to let them come. He wanted to bless them. So if you have to hang out with little kids, be kind. Then you'll remember to do the same even as you grow older.

Jesus, I am blessed that I will get to eat with you when I get to heaven, and I won't have to sit at the kiddy table. Amen.

JESUS NEVER BRAGGED

Jesus called his twelve disciples together and gave them authority to cast out evil spirits and to heal every kind of disease and illness. (Matthew 10:1, NLT)

When Daniel scored a point for his team, he bragged about how good he was and how much the team needed him. Daniel never gave credit to his coach or his other teammates; he wanted all of the glory for himself. Jesus was not like Daniel. Jesus trained and helped his disciples to do the types of things he could do. If he had been selfish and wanted all of the attention, he wouldn't have helped the rest of them perform miracles. But then, when Jesus went back to heaven, there would have been no one to carry on his message. It's a good thing Jesus trained his followers to do great things! When you are good at something, don't hog it to yourself. Use your ability to try to help other people get better, too. God gave you abilities to help others – not to hog them to yourself.

Lord, help me to be selfless and not hog my talents to myself. Amen.

JESUS USED STORIES

Jesus always used stories and illustrations like these when speaking to the crowds. In fact, he never spoke to them without using such parables. (Matthew 13:34, NLT)

When you watch a movie, read a book, or listen to a song, you are learning something through a story. It might be a good lesson. It might be a bad lesson. It might be a dumb lesson. Jesus understood that stories capture people's attention. You can help others learn through your story. One way you can share Jesus with those who don't know him is by sharing your story of how he has helped you and what he means to your life. Take some time and write out what your "God story" would be, and then share it with your friends and family.

God, help me to know what my "God story" is and how to tell it to others. Amen.

JESUS WALKED ON WATER

About three o'clock in the morning Jesus came toward them, walking on the water. (Matthew 14:25, NLT)

Faith is powerful. When you have faith in something, you can do great stuff. Jesus' faith was so great that he could actually walk on water. Peter started to walk on the water, but his faith was weak and he became afraid. The other disciples didn't even get out of the boat! When you have faith in God, he can use you to do mighty things. But if you allow doubt to interfere, it will slow you down. Is your faith strong? Figure out what areas of the Bible you find hard to trust in and ask God to build you up to be a young man of faith.

God, please build up my faith. Point out where my faith is weak and help me to get stronger in those areas. Amen.

JESUS KNEW THE BIBLE

Jesus replied, "And why do you break the command of God for the sake of your tradition?" (Matthew 15:3, NIV)

Some religious leaders questioned Jesus about why he broke traditions, but Jesus pointed out how those religious leaders were hypocrites. This means they made rules for other people that they themselves did not follow. In addition, they were breaking God's commands in order to keep their traditions – and God's commands have more authority. Jesus asked them about Scripture and spoke about how they themselves did not follow God's commands.

Jesus knew Scripture really well. When he was attacked publicly, Jesus could rely on God's word to show the truth. You know it is important to read your Bible, but it is also important to memorize important parts of your Bible. That way, you can remember verses even when you don't have a Bible nearby.

Lord, thank you for your words to me in the Bible. I am going to memorize one verse at a time so that I can get to know your word better every day. Amen.

JESUS WAS BORN IN A STABLE

[Mary] gave birth to her firstborn, a son. She wrapped him in cloths and placed him in a manger, because there was no room for them in the inn. (Luke 2:7, NIV)

Jesus was in heaven before he came to earth to die for your sins. He became a tiny human baby. He wasn't even born as a prince in a palace; instead, he was born to a poor couple who were in an unfamiliar town where there wasn't even room in the inn. Jesus was born in a stable, and Mary used a manger for a cradle. The Bible says, "Though he was God, he did not think of equality with God as something to cling to. Instead, he gave up his divine privileges; he took the humble position of a slave and was born as a human being" (Philippians 2:6-7, NLT). Would you be willing to give up everything you had to save someone else? Jesus gave up everything to come to earth just for you. Are you willing to give something to him in return? How about your heart?

Jesus, forgive me for not remembering all that you did for me. Thank you for coming as a tiny baby so that you could grow up and die for my sins. Amen.

JESUS WAS PRACTICAL

Jesus called his disciples and told them, "I feel sorry for these people. They have been here with me for three days, and they have nothing left to eat. I don't want to send them away hungry, or they will faint along the way." (Matthew 15:32, NLT)

Jesus healed people from bad diseases, cast out demons, and even raised people from the dead. He could do miracles, but he also cared about practical things. Because he was human, he experienced being tired and hungry, so he knew that the people who had been listening to him would need some food before they went home. Then, of course, he supplied food for everyone! Jesus cares about your daily needs. He cares that you have clothes and food, too. Jesus will help you if you do not have something that you really need. When you pray to Jesus, ask him for the things you need, because he cares about your daily needs.

Jesus, please provide for my daily needs. Thank you for caring about me so much! Amen.

JESUS LISTENED TO GOD

Jesus turned to Peter and said, "Get away from me, Satan! You are a dangerous trap to me. You are seeing things merely from a human point of view, not from God's." (Matthew 16:23, NLT)

Timothy was in a one-mile race, and his coach told him not to run too fast at first, but to save his energy. Timothy's friends were cheering and telling him to run faster and faster. So Timothy ignored his coach's advice and he didn't have enough strength to finish the race. If he had listened to his coach, he might have won. Like Timothy's coach, God knows a lot more stuff than you do, so it is important to listen to him. Your friends may be good friends, but they are young and don't know everything yet. Even Jesus couldn't listen to what Peter suggested, for Jesus knew that God had other plans. God has given you the Bible so you know how you are to run the race. Stick with the game plan and listen to the coach – God.

God, I love my friends, but I understand that you know more than they do. Amen.

JESUS WANTS US TO FOLLOW HIM

Jesus said to his disciples, "If any of you wants to be my follower, you must turn from your selfish ways, take up your cross, and follow me." (Matthew 16:24, NLT)

All the cars on a train move because the engine pulls them along the railroad tracks. The other cars don't go in different directions; they just follow their leader, which is the engine. Jesus is your engine. He is the leader, and all you need to do is follow him. If you do follow him, you won't go off the tracks. Jesus wants you to follow his teachings more than anything because he knows that if you do, then you will live a better life on earth. He asks you to take up your cross, and that means to be willing to sacrifice everything for him. When you follow him, not only will you find the life God has planned for you on earth, but you will also one day experience the future he has planned for you in heaven. And what a wonderful place that will be!

Jesus, be my lead engine and keep me from going off track. Amen.

JESUS BELIEVED IN FORGIVENESS

Peter came to Jesus and asked, "Lord, how many times shall I forgive my brother when he sins against me? Up to seven times?" Jesus answered, "I tell you, not seven times, but seventy-seven times." (Matthew 18:21-22, NIV)

How many times have you messed up? The truth is, you probably have made a lot of mistakes in your life. Jesus' disciples asked him how many times they had to forgive someone who sinned against them. Some of them thought seven times would be enough, but Jesus told them they were way off. Jesus told them that you should always be willing to forgive. By saying "seventy-seven times," Jesus was basically saying, "Don't try to keep count – just always forgive." Why? Because Jesus forgives you over and over again, so he wants you to forgive others as many times as they need. One reason Jesus forgives you is so you are able to forgive others. Everyone needs to be forgiven.

Lord, please soften my heart and help me to forgive others. Thank you for forgiving me. Amen.

JESUS WAS ABANDONED

*Jesus told them, "Tonight all of you will
desert me. For the Scriptures say, 'God will
strike the Shepherd, and the sheep of the flock
will be scattered.'" (Matthew 26:31, NLT)*

Even though Jesus had many followers, on the
night that he was arrested, no one stuck with him.
One of his disciples, Judas, had betrayed him to
the religious leaders and then came and, with a
kiss on his cheek, pointed him out to the soldiers.
Then the rest of the disciples ran away and left
him by himself. Later, even his close friend Peter
pretended like he didn't even know who Jesus
was. Jesus was abandoned.

You might have had some tough times in your
life, but don't forget that Jesus had tough times,
too. If your family isn't perfect, or if you feel
alone, or when you wonder if anyone is on your
side, just remember that Jesus is there for you. He
knows how you feel.

Jesus, I'm sorry you felt lonely and were abandoned,
but thank you for being there for me. Amen.

JESUS BELIEVES IN FRESH STARTS

After breakfast Jesus asked Simon Peter, "Simon son of John, do you love me more than these?" "Yes, Lord," Peter replied, "you know I love you." "Then feed my lambs," Jesus told him. (John 21:15, NLT)

After Jesus died on the cross and rose again, he reached out to those who had left him in his hardest time. He prepared breakfast on the beach for the eleven disciples. Then he had a special conversation with Peter, who had denied him. Jesus forgave Peter, and Peter became one of the main leaders of the early church after Jesus returned to heaven. Jesus forgave Peter because Jesus believes in new beginnings. When you follow Jesus, you always get new beginnings if you need them. When one year ends and a new one begins, you can look forward to a new start when the new year comes. If this year has not been the best, then ask God for a new beginning.

God, thank you for this year. Please bless this next year. I want to work with you to make it the best one I have ever had. Amen.

JAYCE O'NEAL is an author and actor who enjoys cheering for his favorite sports teams while eating pizza with a fork. He likes to watch movies, visit amusement parks, and play board games. Jayce has a big heart for ministry, truth, and love. He also just downright enjoys being creative and encouraging others to use their imagination. He has a Doctorate, two Master's Degrees, a Bachelor of Science, and a small trophy for perfect attendance in Sunday school from when he was nine. He currently resides with his fantabulous wife in the Los Angeles area.